choosing and keeping

ducks and
geese

choosing and keeping

ducks and geese

Liz Wright

PUBLISHED BY

TFH Publications, Inc.
One TFH Plaza
Third and Union Avenues
Neptune City, NJ 07753

ISBN 978-0-7938-0668-3

Printed and bound in Dubai
08 09 10 11 12 1 3 5 7 9 8 6 4 2

Library of Congress Cataloging-in-Publication Data
Wright, Liz.
  Choosing and keeping ducks and geese / Liz Wright.
    p. cm.
  Includes index.
  ISBN 978-0-7938-0668-3 (alk. paper)
  1. Ducks. 2. Geese. I. Title.

SF505W78 2008
636.5'97—dc22

2008010431

The Leader in Responsible Animal Care
for Over 50 Years!®
www.tfh.com

Contents

Introduction

It's easier than you might think to keep ducks and geese, and very rewarding. But how do you get started and what breeds should you choose? Read on to enter the wonderful world of waterfowl.

Why keep ducks and geese?

You've thought about keeping some waterfowl. So, should you take the next step?
Ducks and geese certainly make delightful, colorful, and characterful additions to the
household, but they are also useful.

Above Ducks also make great pets, especially for children.

Ducks

Some duck breeds produce large quantities of big,
creamy eggs. In 1918, E.A. Taylor wrote in his book
Runner Ducks that Indian Runners could produce
200 or more eggs per year, with six eggs weighing
1 lb (450 g). He felt that the future of the duck as an
egg layer in comparison to a hen was assured. Some
duck breeds were developed for meat and back in
1885, William Cook asserted in his well-known *Poultry
Breeder and Feeder* that "in a few years duck-keeping
will become a general thing." Although neither of
these predictions came true, eggs and meat still
remain important reasons for keeping ducks.

Ducks have other uses as well:

They can assist you in clearing your garden of
slugs and snails, thereby reducing the number of
hungry mouths that make it to your precious plants.
However, you will need to keep them away from some
vegetables, such as lettuce and other salad greens,
that they find particularly tasty.

Ducks also make good pets – little Call ducks are
particularly suitable for children as they are easy to
handle and can become very tame (see pages
102–104). Used from around 150 years ago as
decoys to lure wildfowl into man-made traps, their
nosey and noisy nature lets you know when there
are strangers or predators about.

Some ducks are kept solely for their beauty. These
include the wild Mandarin (see pages 194–197)
and the domestic Rouen (see pages 150–151), once
bred for the table and now prized for its wonderful
markings. Duck plumage is particularly stunning and

Above Ducks are fantastic for keeping slugs and snails off plants. This wine label states "Ducks are employed to keep the grape vines free from snails. They are far more efficient and eco-friendly than harmful chemicals."

in many breeds is also iridescent – black feathers especially often have a beetle-green sheen. Crested varieties add to the appeal.

Geese

Geese were traditionally bred for meat. Their ability to forage and fatten mainly on grass makes them economical birds to rear, although good grazing is essential. While not renowned for laying, some breeds can produce between 60 and 100 eggs per year. These very large eggs are wonderful to eat but are also sought after by artists for decoration. The art of painting on eggs or applying other materials to produce a colourful craft was made famous by Fabergé, whose fabulous creations for the Russian court in the late nineteenth century provide the inspiration for a hobby that still has a strong following today.

Geese are also useful for other purposes:

Goose (and duck) down is popular for pillows and duvets and is unashamedly associated with luxury.

It is perhaps as sentinels that geese excel. Exceptionally intelligent birds, they are often kept as guards for property as they are very alert – and few people are keen to pass through a flock of loudly honking geese! The birds have been kept for this purpose for many centuries, perhaps from as early as 309 BC when they were credited with saving Rome from attack by the Gauls.

Geese (and ducks) are also useful in controlling weed growth on the banks of rivers and ponds, as well as underwater weeds. Geese are grazers and so are great for keeping the grass down, especially in places the lawnmower cannot reach such as ditches and orchards. They'll also clear up fruit that has fallen, which might attract wasps if left to rot.

Exhibition

Both ducks and geese can be kept for exhibition purposes (see pages 90–97). There are classes for them at most poultry shows as well as specialist shows for waterfowl. Showing is a sociable activity where people of like mind can meet, talk, and compare birds.

You can keep ducks and geese for a combination of any of the above reasons. They can also provide you with hours fun just watching their activities and some breeds will become quite tame. The sound of quacking or honking quickly becomes music to the ears of the enthusiastic owner. Ducks and geese are truly versatile birds and will repay you time and time again in many ways for your care of them.

Introduction

Ducks and geese through history

Egyptians were keeping geese over 4,000 years ago and excavations have shown they were incubating goose eggs artificially in the sand. There is also evidence that ancient peoples had been trapping geese in the Nile Delta long before this time.

Ancient ancestors

The main ancestor of domestic geese in Europe is the Greylag, still seen today as a migratory bird. This is the largest of the wild geese in Europe, weighing up to 12 lb (5.5 kg), and has gray-brown plumage which is barred on the back and belly. In flight, it has a striking blue-gray panel on the leading edge of the inner wing.

It is thought that Chinese geese originated from the wild Asiatic Swan goose, perhaps so-named for its long neck. This is smaller than the Greylag, weighing up to 6½ lb (3 kg). It has a long, heavy black bill, chestnut-brown cap with a similar broad stripe down the back of the neck, and pale underparts with some belly streaking. Along with many other species, loss of habitat has reduced its numbers.

Roman influences

The Romans were keen on geese and used them as guards, but they also reared them for meat and feathers. Pliny writes about force feeding geese to swell the liver: he credits his contemporary, Roman gastronome Marcus Gavius Apicus, with feeding them dried figs for this purpose. The practice of force feeding still takes place today to produce *pâté de foie gras*, much to the concern of animal welfare organizations. The Romans went on to develop a white goose.

To their surprise, the invaders found that the early Britons did not eat geese although they kept them. Goose then gradually became part of the diet, perhaps under Roman influence. Certainly geese were a common sight in Europe by the first century AD, when the first reports of moving flocks with their feet protected by coverings are found – in this case, across the Alps. The goose was already domesticated worldwide.

Ducks and domestication

Ducks, too, had a connection to humankind in ancient times, but initially mainly as wild birds that were hunted rather than domesticated. Amazingly, the common Mallard duck is thought to be the ancestor of all domestic ducks apart from the Muscovy.

The Muscovy duck is sometimes mistaken for a goose, probably due to its unique habit of "hissing"

Above Amazingly, all domestic ducks except the Muscovy are descended from the Mallard.

instead of quacking, which no other duck displays. It is descended from a tree duck and as a result has very strong claws. Due to continued good nutrition in domestication, the breed has developed into a much larger and heavier bird than its ancestor.

Experts have different opinions on whether the goose or the duck was the first domesticated bird, but all agree that one of these was domesticated prior to the chicken. Variations in the size and type of ducks and geese came about through developing genetic mutations, selective breeding and domestication over a very long period.

The Middle Ages

Duck and goose keeping continued to spread as the centuries rolled on. In Europe, by the Middle Ages geese were being kept for meat, eggs and feathers. They were raised as "green geese," killed at 12–16 weeks old, or were dispatched in late autumn as "stubble geese." Goose remains from Winchester Abbey in Hampshire and Eynsham Abbey in Oxfordshire studied by archaeologists show evidence of the use of feathers for quill pens.

At this time, geese were regarded as being as useful as pigs. As well as meat and eggs, they provided quills for writing and arrow making, and grease for use in medicine for poultices, keeping leather supple, and protecting the hooves, paws, feet, and ears of animals and people in extreme cold weather.

The tradition of eating goose at Christmas, Michaelmas (September 29), and Pentecost gradually evolved. Today, Goose Fairs are still held in early autumn, many having been revived relatively recently. The Feast of St. Martin celebrated on November 11 in mainland Europe also sees goose on the menu. Legend has it that in 371 AD St. Martin, feeling that he was unworthy to replace the Bishop of Tours, hid in a goose pen but loudly cackling geese gave him away. A fifteenth-century folksong, "The Fox and the Goose," is still sung in parts of Europe today.

Introduction

Above Champion winning Toulouse gander in 1934.

Ducks were increasingly domesticated and feature in many monastery and abbey records, including those of Ramsey Abbey in Cambridgeshire: these describe "cirrar" ducks, which may mean "crested." It is difficult to quantify from such records the value of the wild ducks that were widely available.

Meanwhile, the duck continued to thrive worldwide. Numbers were strong in China and Indonesia, where breeds developed differently – in particular, with more upright carriage – to those in Europe and North Africa. The names often give them away: the Pekin duck, for example, obviously originated in China.

Ducks and geese were very much part of medieval life, being relatively easy to rear, providing meat throughout the winter, the important grease and fat for a variety of uses, and feathers for warm bedding.

Seventeenth–twentieth century

The goose also played a part in the English Civil War (1624–1649), where being in the Brotherhood of the Grey Goose Feather was to show allegiance to the King rather than Parliament, and guaranteed safe passage through the watery East of England. It was not uncommon for family members and neighbors to be on opposing sides, hence the need for a discreet method of showing loyalty.

Duck was now firmly on the menu all around the world. In 1685, Robert May wrote in *The Accomplisht Cook* of a special feast consisting of "Three ducks, one larded" and "Powdered Geese."

By this time, wild ducks were being trapped in large numbers using decoys, and by the nineteenth century Decoy ducks – what we now know as Call ducks – were being used to entice wild ducks into a pool covered by a trap. These came from Holland and were also known as Dutch Call ducks, although it is thought they originated from Asia and arrived in Holland via trading routes. Hunters sometimes referred to a gathering of ducks as a "badelynge of ducks."

Drovers' routes, which were used to move stock from grazing areas to market, saw flocks of geese with their feet covered as in ancient times herded into the Christmas markets. Ducks, too, were walked – to water by day, returning to safety at night. At Builth Wells in Powys, Wales, there is a plaque commemorating this in the appropriately named Duck Lane.

By the late nineteenth and into the early twentieth century, ducks and geese were widespread in the UK as indispensable sources of meat, eggs, feathers, and grease. "Goose clubs" sprang up, where families paid a few pence a week from early autumn to buy a goose for Christmas dinner – a forerunner of the modern Christmas clubs.

In the US, no homestead or farm was complete without guard geese, which also supplied these other material benefits. Just as they had been for the early settlers, geese were part of a self-sufficient lifestyle – one that is being reclaimed by many people today. *The White House Cook Book*, published in 1903, provides a menu for a Christmas feast that includes "Roast Goose, Apple Sauce, Boiled Potatoes, Mashed Turnips, Creamed Parsnips, Stewed Onions, Boiled Rice, Lobster Salad, Canvas Back Duck."

The cult of Mother Goose became important in the US, too, her image synonymous with that of an idealistic childhood. Mother Goose had first appeared in a book of nursery rhymes published in London in 1780, but passed into American literature with Isaiah Thomas's reprint in 1786. Various publishers continued with the trend, with McLoughlin – a prolific nineteenth-century company – issuing ever cheaper and more colorful versions.

Profitable waterfowl

In the late nineteenth century, famous poultryman William Cook was saying that "geese are but little kept in many parts of the country as the majority of farmers think they are very unprofitable." But he also asserted that "they have paid me as well as any other poultry I have ever kept." The disadvantage, he believed, was that they make so much noise. He believed they should

Above Khaki Campbell ducks were specially bred to produce large numbers of good-sized eggs.

be grazed "where land is cheap" and maintained that they "pay better than sheep."

Utility Poultry Farming for Australasia, billed in 1908 as "a Book for the Man with 6 birds or 6,000," talked of "poultry plants marketing 50,000 ducks" for meat and mentioned "prime young ducks realizing a profit of 1/- per head," which was not a bad amount of profit at all for the time.

In 1918, E.A. Taylor, writing about the Indian Runner as "a forager and egg duck," confidently stated that "in the near future when its value is fully known to farmers, Small Holders and all interested in egg-production, it will be stocked in preference to the hen." He could not have envisaged the battery production of hens' eggs that was to come, a system that is totally unsuited to ducks.

In 1933, *Poultry and Poultry Husbandry* magazine carried photographs of ducks in a garden close to Crystal Palace and asserted that before World War I there were many small duck farms alongside rivers. A cover shot showed a flock of Aylesbury and Indian Runner ducks and was captioned: "A profitable section of livestock kept on the establishment." While acknowledging that ducks could be reared intensively, geese were still considered best for grazing and "finding almost the whole of their food."

Duck egg production became important in both the UK and US before and during World War II, with books and journals claiming an unbelievable average of 300 eggs for backyard ducks and stating that this was "not uncommon."

Exhibition birds

In the late nineteenth century, the hobby of poultry showing became popular in the UK and US, and ducks and geese began to be seen as exhibition birds. The hobby grew in strength, and farmers and smallholders often kept a few extra birds specifically for exhibition while keen hobbyists strove to breed for color and type, "improving" old breeds and developing new ones.

Ducks and Disney

During World War II, the Disney studio was responsible for drawing some of the ducks that appeared in US military insignia - and, of course, Donald Duck appeared in his fair share of wartime cartoons.

Both World Wars took their toll, but showing resumed afterwards. However, in later years the numbers of farmers and smallholders keeping ducks and geese, and therefore showing them, began to drop due to the increasing intensification of poultry farming (see pages 90–97).

Decline and revival

Duck and goose keeping declined from the 1960s onwards worldwide, with the growing preference for chicken and its low price, which made it available to most families. Geese had long been overtaken as the Christmas bird by turkey.

However, the 1980s saw a revival in self-sufficient living which has continued to gather momentum. Goose is becoming increasingly popular once again at Christmas and duck meat has made a comeback. The scares surrounding food poisoning traced to duck eggs in the 1930s and 1940s have been all but forgotten as more hygienic production and careful cooking (they should be hardboiled) have overcome the problem. Duck eggs are once again becoming sought after and are stocked in most large supermarkets.

Now, in the twenty-first century, people are keeping ducks and geese for all the reasons that our ancestors found so enticing. In addition, many who keep them are not afraid to admit that they also keep these delightful birds simply as pets, to enjoy.

Which breed?

Successful duck or goose keeping starts with choosing the right breed for your particular circumstances and needs. There are many varieties available, all with their own special appeal. Visiting a poultry show may help you to make your choice.

What your waterfowl want from you

It's important that you get to know the characteristics of the many breeds and that you are clear about the care and facilities you can offer. Time spent now making a careful choice is well worth the effort. Details of a wide range of ducks and geese are provided in the Breeds Directory (see pages 98–199).

Water

This should be your first consideration. All ducks and geese need some form of water for preening – at the

Above Geese need plenty of space and grass.

very least, they must be able to get their heads into water to clean their eyes and nostrils. Most breeds can manage very well with mobile containers that can be washed out or a purpose-made concrete pond. The golden rule is not to overstock, as web feet and dabbling beaks will make a confined area very muddy and the birds will soon foul small volumes of water. Some breeds can only be considered if you have have access to a large pond, lake, or river. Because there are so many different types, it should be possible to find a breed that is suitable for your situation. For more details, see pages 34–37.

Space

The smaller ducks, such as bantams or Call ducks, are suitable for small gardens (but remember that there is good reason for the "Call" in their name!). All ducks and geese need space and do not do well if they are kept in cramped conditions, so make sure you don't overstock. It is a good idea to start with just a few birds to see how well your plot copes with the new arrivals. Geese really need access to grass, although they are sometimes kept as house pets and guard geese in smaller gardens, but management such as cleaning out and feeding must be adjusted accordingly. An area of concrete or slabs will help as you can keep it clean by hosing down, but bear in mind that ducks naturally "dabble" and geese love to graze so you should consider these behaviors when you assess your land. It might be practical to have a couple of enclosures, so that one can be shut off to recover while the other is in use. For more details, see pages 28–33.

Time

Although ducks and geese are relatively easy to care for, time must be allowed for shutting them in at night to protect them against foxes and other predators and letting them out again the morning, *every* day. If you cannot commit to this, you will need to provide a genuinely predator-proof pen with a good-sized run (see pages 38–39). In addition, you will have to spend time keeping the area clean and, if your ponds are small, changing the water. With egg-laying breeds you will need to collect the eggs daily to ensure cleanliness.

The more time you can spend with your birds, the better – as well as being pleasurable, watching them will give you early indication of anything that may be wrong. If you are planning to breed, you will have to devote more time to ensuring this is successful (and will also need separate pens, and somewhere to keep incubators and rear youngsters) – see pages 72–89.

Knowledge and experience

Those who are new to ducks and geese are embarking on an enjoyable undertaking – there is so much to discover every day in the delightful way they behave. However, a basic knowledge of their care is a must before you purchase, and some breeds are much easier for first timers to keep than others. Wildfowl require a greater level of knowledge than domestic birds, and some domestic breeds need more care than others. For example, Sebastopol geese with their curled, white feathers can easily become very dirty without access to water and their plumage can suffer through normal but lively behavior if they are kept with other breeds of geese. The golden rule is: start with a small number of ducks or geese from a breed that it is easy to keep.

What you want from your waterfowl

Because every breed has been developed to fulfill a particular purpose, you also need to think about what you want from your birds, as this will influence your choice. Of course, it is very likely that even if you keep ducks or geese for one purpose such as eggs, you will find several other reasons as well – which will almost certainly include their beauty and character.

Eggs

Duck eggs have a really rich flavor with a strong, orange yolk and are usually larger than a hen's egg – in many cases, much larger. People who like them seek them out and they do command a higher price than hen's eggs (if you have any spare after you and your family have eaten them!). They are wonderful in baking and often impart a lovely color to biscuits and cakes. Otherwise, they should always be hardboiled.

A free-ranging duck of an appropriate breed such as Khaki Campbell, Abacot Ranger, or Welsh Harlequin

The Five Freedoms

In most countries, it is agreed that all farmed animals and birds should enjoy the "Five Freedoms":

Freedom from hunger and thirst with ready access to fresh water and a diet to maintain full health and vigor.

Freedom from discomfort by provision of an appropriate environment including shelter and a comfortable resting area.

Freedom from pain, injury, or disease through prevention or rapid diagnosis and treatment.

Freedom to express normal behavior by provision of sufficient space, proper facilities, and company of the animal's own kind.

Freedom from fear and distress by ensuring conditions and care that avoid mental suffering.

Above A Khaki Campbell may lay up to 300 eggs a year.

may lay up to 300 eggs per year, while Indian Runners easily lay up to 200. Even a Rouen Clair, a table duck now prized for exhibition, can turn in a respectable average of around 150. Bantam ducks generally lay fewer eggs per year. However, whatever the breed you also have to take into account the strain: do your ducks come from a line of birds that laid large numbers of eggs? One of the reasons hens were developed for egg laying ahead of ducks is because the latter require more food; on the plus side, if your ducks have a decent area to range around in they will find a lot for themselves as well as ridding your land of many pests.

Geese are not renowned for laying large numbers of eggs, although Chinese geese are competent layers. The larger breeds such as Embdens lay very large eggs, often weighing 6–8 oz (175–225 g) each – and these are large enough to make a delicious one-egg omelette. Goose eggs are also in demand for decoration (see page 9).

Meat
Both ducks and geese have always been raised for the table. A commercial duck (often a Pekin/Aylesbury cross) is quick growing and will weigh 7¾ lb (3.5 kg) at 49 days. If they go beyond this they become difficult to pluck, due to the change of feathers at this time from juvenile to adult. Purebreds mature more slowly, the time taken depending on the breed.

If you are considering rearing ducks for the table, the most important requirement is that you are able to slaughter humanely and quickly, and then pluck and dress the carcass. Do not even contemplate raising table birds if you find this distasteful. The same goes for geese, which are large birds to slaughter. In many countries they are once more gaining popularity as gourmet dining for Christmas, so they are in demand. The other requirement for producing table birds is therefore to ensure you have a market, as you will need to take orders before they are killed.

Pets
Because of their delightful nature, ducks and geese make good pets. If you have reared them from young, they will have no fear of humans and will come to you.

By nature ducks are not aggressive creatures, which adds to the pleasure of keeping them. Geese can make good pets but these birds can sometimes be aggressive. Often this is displayed most obviously during the breeding season, when the gander becomes possessive and defensive.

For both ducks and geese, it is generally better to choose a domesticated rather than wildfowl breed to keep for pets.

Garden helpers
Ducks are good gardeners as they love to eat slugs and snails. The downside is that they also enjoy many of the crops, especially salad greens and berries. A good plan is to fence the vegetable plot but allow the ducks access around the edge to pick off a large proportion of the pests. You can also allow them on to the garden after harvest and in the winter. Indian Runners are a particularly good choice for this as they are a comparatively light breed. Geese have a good reputation as "weeders" and can be

used to control plants along fences and around buildings. Obviously they won't know weeds from wanted plants, so your management must be geared towards achieving the aim. Geese are great in orchards to keep grass down and clear up windfalls. Other grazing animals would chew the trees but geese do only good.

Exhibition

If you would like to exhibit your ducks or geese, first visit a show or two to see what goes on and talk to some of the exhibitors. If you decide to go ahead, you will need to join the appropriate breed club or waterfowl association. You will need your birds to be fairly tame, so that as you breed youngsters you can handle them with future shows in mind.

Poultry showing is an inexpensive hobby and entry fees are relatively low; the biggest expense is travel. It's also a very social hobby: the birds penned early in the morning leaving you free to meet up with other exhibitors and assess the competition. There are often special juvenile classes as well, so the whole family can become involved if they wish to. For more details, see pages 90–97.

Above Indian Runners, being a light breed make good gardeners.

Above Geese are not always renowned for being good layers, but Chinese geese are competent.

Sheepducks

Occasionally, ducks and geese are worked by sheepdogs in displays. The natural flocking instinct of Indian Runners make them naturals for this. It is important that they are not ducks in lay, and drakes are normally preferred.

Guard geese

All through history, geese have been used to alert people to danger. They are constantly on the lookout, and if anything unusual happens or someone passes their pen they honk loudly. Chinese geese are particularly effective in this role. Many people are as nervous about passing geese as they are a guard dog.

Just for fun

Sit and watch your ducks dabbling in a pond or a puddle, their tails wagging furiously, their heads and bodies making fluid movements as they preen. Admire the plumage of geese against green grass and observe them interact with each other. You can literally spend hours just watching your birds and you'll feel more relaxed for it. All breeds are good to watch and have their own special attractions.

Preserving rare breeds

Surprisingly, the best known breeds of ducks and geese are actually the most rare. Breeds we take for granted, that have been part of a country's history, are now the breeds where true specimens are hard to find.

Introduction

Under threat

The Aylesbury duck – the large, white meat-producing duck that everyone recognizes – is rare in every country. It appears on the Australian list of top ten priority breeds and as critical in the American Livestock Breeds Conservancy list. New Zealand, too, lists it as rare, citing the fact that eating duck is not particularly popular in that country. In the UK, where the breed originated, the big exhibition strain is extremely rare but makes an impressive sight when you do get to see it.

The Embden goose, another well-known breed, is also on the top ten priority list in Australia, while the American Livestock Breeds Conservancy are concerned

about two breeds particularly associated with the US: the American Buff and the Pilgrim, whose status is again described as critical. The Pilgrim is also rare in New Zealand, as is the Cape Barren goose which is a threatened species in its native Australia. This is an unusual bird whose closest relative is not a goose but the New Zealand Paradise Shelduck.

The Shetland goose, a breed not unlike the Pilgrim, has very few bloodlines in the US and is listed as critical. In the UK, too, the numbers are very low. Although descended in pure isolation on Shetland from the very oldest of stock, the breed came close to extinction in modern times. However, the birds made it from Shetland to the rest of the UK, the US, and Canada, where ironically numbers are probably higher than in their native land. There is also a black Shetland duck, a lively and hardy breed with a liking for water that is credited with keeping down liver fluke thanks to its ravenous foraging on the islands.

Why do breeds become rare?

Breeds of waterfowl often fall out of fashion when they do not meet the commercial needs of the time or new commercial breeds are developed that lay more and put on more weight, more quickly. They may also adapt better to intensive conditions – for example, a breed that had to be able to walk the drovers' roads may be unable to cope with living close together in a single shed.

Yet we need to retain the genes of these breeds. A commercial bird is developed from original pure breeds, selected for a variety of characteristics. If we

Above The Aylesbury, once prolific, is now hard to find in its true form.

lose a breed, we lose the genes that make it what it is and we have no "gene bank" for the future. It is difficult to predict what type of bird will be needed in, say, 50 years' time: no doubt the breeders of the classic Aylesbury thought that this was the bird for the future, only to have it fall out of favor. Climate change, new consumer demands for slower-maturing, leaner meat, commercial pressures for faster growing, higher egg layers – who knows what we will require of the duck or goose in years to come?

Preserving the future

Ironically, these heritage breeds are not only our past, but also possibly our future. We owe it to the people who carefully bred them, sometimes hundreds of years ago, to preserve their vision in its purest form. The difficulties are often the lack of sufficient bloodlines – which will ultimately cause problems in fertility, among other things – and the need for specialist conditions. Birds that adapt to a commercial way of keeping tend to survive, while those that need water to mate or other special facilities that make them harder to keep lose ground.

If you have the interest and the time, and can provide the right conditions, do keep a rare breed going. You will be providing a service not only to the birds themselves but also to future generations of people, who will not only still have great breeds of the past to marvel over but also important gene pools for the future.

Above Why not keep a rare breed, like the American Buff, not only for yourself but for the benefit of future generations.

Getting Started

So, you have now decided that ducks or geese are definitely for you – but don't just rush out to buy some birds. Good facilities and equipment will make keeping your waterfowl more pleasurable for you and much better for them. This chapter explains everything you need to have ready before you get your birds.

Equipment

You do not need many items of equipment to keep your waterfowl healthy and content, but whatever you use should be suitable for the purpose and easy to clean. Understanding the needs of your birds will help you to make the correct choices.

Feeders

It is not a good idea to throw feed straight on to the ground for waterfowl. They will paddle it into the mud and spoil it with droppings, and the waste will encourage vermin.

For ducks and geese, a trough that cannot be tipped over is the first choice. You can buy purpose-made designs, but an old, clean pig trough is another good choice. Small numbers of birds will do well with the shallow rubber feed bowls used to feed ponies. Plastic is fine too, but the design must be robust enough to withstand heavy birds perching on the side.

All ducks must be able to feed at once, so there should be enough troughs or bowls of an appropriate size to accommodate the entire flock. This is not really an issue with geese, as they mostly graze and flocks tend to be smaller. Moving the troughs from time to time will prevent the ground around the base becoming soiled. Troughs and bowls must be easy to clean and to empty: never put fresh food on top of waste food as it will become sour and the birds won't eat it anyway.

Also available are self-feeding hoppers that allow more grain to drop down as the birds eat and have a lid to protect the supply. Auto-feeders provide a self-operating system: as the birds peck at the tag under the feeder, it releases a small quantity of pellets or wheat.

Above Self-feeding food containers keep feed clean until it drops down to be eaten.

Above Grit needs to be fed in a strong bowl.

Left Auto-feeders have a self-operating tag system, perfect for free-range birds.

23

Getting Started

Originally designed for feeding pheasants in woods, it has become useful for free-range poultry and waterfowl as it discourages contact from wild birds and vermin. This type of feeder may also help to prevent feather plucking and boredom because the bird is actively searching for food.

Grit should be fed in a strong trough or bowl and be freely available (see Feeding, pages 50–53).

Storage

You need to consider how to store your feed. Bagged feed attracts vermin and should therefore be kept in a secure bin. Rats can eat through plastic if they are hungry, so a metal bin is ideal. A secure feed bin is a good investment as it also keeps feed clean and dry.

You can buy purpose-made feed scoops, or give discarded saucepans from the kitchen a final home in the feed bin.

A small, lockable cupboard is useful for storing feed additives, veterinary medicines, and equipment such as scissors, especially if your waterfowl area is some distance from the house.

Water containers

These must be heavy enough not to tip over easily and also large enough for the birds to be able to submerge their heads and necks. Rubber buckets and trugs are suitable, but the design must be stable. They must be easy to clean out, as must a shallow pond. A purpose-made, molded plastic duck pond will last a long time, but a plastic children's pool can also be used. The criteria are that it is stable when the ducks or geese are using it and that it is easy for the birds to get in and out of. For more details about providing water for ducks and geese, see pages 34–37.

Acquiring stock

You've been to shows and sales, you've read up on the breeds, and now you are ready to go out and get started with your own birds. There are a number of possible sources of good birds, each with advantages and disadvantages.

Breeders are best

The best way to buy any stock is to go directly to a respected breeder – contact the secretary of the relevant breed club for a list of breeders in your area. The next step is to contact the breeders to see if they have stock available and make an appointment to see them. At some times of year the birds you want might not be available, so be patient. You can take the opportunity anyway to meet the breeder, review their

Above Let ducks acclimatize to their new home when they arrive.

stock, and discuss your requirements for the future. There is a great deal to be learned from an expert showing you their birds. You can ask all the questions you need, and if you tell them exactly what you want to do with your birds they can find the right match for you.

Although breeders aim for perfection, not all their stock will succeed on the show bench, so if showing is not your aim you can buy some very good birds that aren't quite exhibition standard relatively inexpensively. If you do want to exhibit or breed, then you will need to spend more to buy a suitable breeding pair or trio (one male and one or two females). An investment in good stock is money well spent and will repay you in the future. It is much more difficult (if not impossible) to upgrade breeding from poor stock than to breed good birds from quality parents.

When buying, remember that males will live together quite peaceably as long as there are no females around and they are often surplus to requirements so are relatively easy and inexpensive to acquire. If you don't want eggs or future generations, you may be happy to have a bachelor group.

Sales and auctions

Many poultry exhibitions and shows have sales attached and these can provide some excellent examples of stock from genuine breeders – but there are also sales where older stock are passed off as young birds, parasites and even disease abound, and birds that don't lay are sold to make some quick cash.

Above Handle new arrivals with care when putting them into their new home.

One of the problems in buying from a sale or auction is that you often come home with something completely different to your original plans, simply because it caught your eye or perhaps you felt sorry for it.

If you buy from a sale or auction, choose a reputable one where the seller declares their name. Don't buy anything that looks sick or sorry, that is limping or is losing feathers – contact your local animal welfare organization if you are concerned.

You will need to be clear about how the breed you have chosen should look – you can carry a picture with you to remind you. Birds are sometimes passed off as a particular breed even if they look only vaguely similar and these may be crossbred. You don't need purebred waterfowl to have fun with them, but if that's what you want and your purchase is not correctly bred, that's not a great start to keeping ducks or geese. If you are uncertain about a pen of birds, trust your judgement despite what the seller tells you and if in doubt leave them alone. If you buy from a sale and already have stock at home, make sure you have an isolation area ready for the new birds where they can remain for at least two weeks. Even though birds may look perfectly healthy they could be incubating a disease or even carrying external parasite.

Advertisements

Farming magazines and local newspapers usually carry advertisements for ducks and geese. As with sales, when you go to look at birds you will have to decide for yourself whether the stock are as advertised, how old they are, and whether they are healthy and of good quality. For example, a seller may genuinely believe that a bird is of a certain breed – perhaps they themselves were sold it as such – but you may think it is no such thing. In that case, walk away and don't buy.

On the web

Using the Internet to research your breed will give you access to a lot of information in a short time. Searching for something as simple as "waterfowl for sale" will bring up breeder directories, breed club sales lists, and auction sales, plus some advertisement sites. It is best to see the birds for yourself before making a purchase – it's more difficult to reject something that has already been delivered, although you have the right to do so if it is not as described in the advertisement.

Be sure to obtain as much information as possible prior to purchase and don't be shy of asking questions.

Getting Started

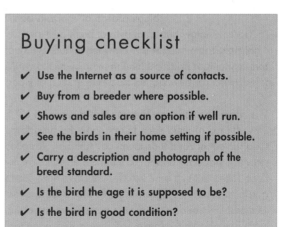

Buying checklist

✔ **Use the Internet as a source of contacts.**

✔ **Buy from a breeder where possible.**

✔ **Shows and sales are an option if well run.**

✔ **See the birds in their home setting if possible.**

✔ **Carry a description and photograph of the breed standard.**

✔ **Is the bird the age it is supposed to be?**

✔ **Is the bird in good condition?**

Young or old?

As well as deciding on a suitable breed for your first venture, you will also have to choose whether to go for ducklings or goslings, or fully grown birds. Youth and maturity both have pros and cons, so you will need to work out which is right for you.

Baby birds

Although young ducklings or goslings are very appealing and cheaper to buy, they do require more specialized care than older birds, as well as the right equipment. You will have to make sure everything is ready for their arrival so that you can keep them warm, as their down will not fulfill this function even at normal temperatures. In addition, at an early age you will probably not be able to sex the birds, so you run the risk of there being too many males when they grow up. (See pages 74–89.)

The advantage of choosing ducklings or goslings is that if they are handled when small they can become very tame and even imprint on people. Of course, as with any young birds or animals you have to be very gentle and not over-handle them, giving them plenty of time to rest (see pages 46–49). However, be careful how you go about this as you may not appreciate a fully grown gander that has become powerfully attached to you, the person who reared him, and believes his place is in your home rather than his own pen!

Young adults

Generally, it is far better to choose young adults as your first waterfowl, as you can see exactly what you

Left Goslings are appealing but it is difficult to tell males and females apart.

are getting and they have been reared to an age where they are less vulnerable. The ideal age would be from around three months for ducklings and four months for geese. They will still have plenty of growing to do and are young enough to adapt to your routine. The birds will be at the beginning of their adult lives and you will not have too long to wait for eggs: ducks will be on the "point of lay" at 21–24 weeks, depending on the time of year, while geese will lay in their first year. Ducks can live for around eight to ten years while a light breed gander can still breed at 20 years of age, so your birds will be with you for many years.

Older birds

Do not rule out older birds completely. For example, a two-year-old goose will be starting to have success in laying and breeding; she will have laid in her first year, but generally the eggs are smaller then and she may not have been successful in raising goslings. An older gander will have his personality fixed, so if he is exhibiting a calm and placid personality it is likely that he will stay that way, unless you change his lifestyle drastically. Ducks carry on laying for most of their lives, although egg production will decrease with age, but a three-year-old duck will still be wanting to lay and rear ducklings, and may well be quite an experienced breeder.

Accidental acquistions

Even with the very best of intentions, you may find yourself in possession of something quite different than your planned stock and very much older or younger, if friends kindly give you surplus birds or you make an impulse buy. If this happens, you will need to learn as much as possible about how to care for your new waterfowl, as quickly as possible – with ducklings and goslings, you have to get it right immediately as they are much more delicate than older birds and need knowledgeable care.

Age checklist

✔ **The younger the bird, the more care it needs.**

✔ **It is usually best to purchase young adults.**

✔ **Ducks and geese have a reasonable lifespan, so do not rule out older birds completely.**

✔ **With young adults and older birds, keep the number of males well below the number of females.**

Above An older duck or goose may already be an experienced layer.

Male or female?

When buying birds, it is important to get the ratio of males to females right for the sake of the females' welfare, as drakes have a powerful sexual appetite. You need only one drake for up to ten ducks – never keep more drakes than ducks. With geese, more than one gander leads to competition. You can keep drakes as pets and they will live together happily as long as you don't introduce any females. You can also keep ducks without a drake and they will still lay eggs.

Planning your facilities

Now is the time to make the final plans for the arrival of your new ducks or geese, so that everything is ready for them in good time. At this stage, it's all about finding the perfect location for them – and for you.

Assess your site

Well before the birds arrive, you should take a long, hard look at the area where you intend to keep them. There may be no choice, because you have a permanent pond or access to a stream for them already, but you will still need to consider where to site the house and enclosure.

It is very important for waterfowl to have plenty of space, and free range if this is practical. If not, they will still need plenty of room in which to move about and a choice of runs, at least one in use and another to shut off for freshening up.

Outdoor life

If you are planning to confine your ducks or geese, make sure that in the summer there will be some shade provision in each of the runs and/or site them out of full sun. Remember that the birds will produce a relatively large quantity of excrement, so ensure there is some hardstanding ground in the form of slabs or concrete that can be cleaned off regularly. They will need at least sufficient depth of water to be able to submerge their heads and necks, and preferably some kind of shallow pond, which needs to be set up so that it can be emptied and cleaned easily.

Grass runs will soon become muddy unless you have enough land to include several and strictly rotate them. It helps to have an outdoor dry surface, perhaps around a pond, created by slabs with sand on top to make them less hard on the birds' feet. Geese love to graze, so an orchard or reasonable-sized paddock would be perfect for them. Check your

Above Take a good look at what is available on your land.

Above A fixed, predator-sage fence encloses a well planned area.

Left An ideal pond with shady trees surrounds a predator-proof fence.

29

soil type and how well it drains: free-draining soil will be better for ducks and geese than heavy clay or a low-lying, naturally wet area which will quickly become a mud bath.

Perhaps the ideal solution is to allow your birds free range during the day and shut them in their house at night, but this will depend on how many predators such as foxes, coyotes, or dogs there are in your area. A fixed, predator-safe run is useful even for free-range birds: there will always be times when they need to be confined, such as if you have to go out for the day and can't get back in time to shut them in.

Siting the bird house

When planning the position of the bird house, first make sure that it will not receive full early morning sun – otherwise in summer you will be getting out of bed earlier to let the birds out so that they don't become overheated. In order that your ducks or geese don't wake your neighbors at the crack of dawn – the birds can be quite noisy when they are waiting to be let out – site their house closer to yours than your neighbors'.

You will be caring for your birds in all weathers, so make sure their house is easily accessible: it's one thing to stroll through low trees and long grass to reach them on a fine summer's day, but quite another in the pouring rain or gloomy dusk of midwinter. A good path to the bird house is pretty much essential.

The house should be built on a hard, solid base, ideally with slabs or concrete immediately around it. This will prevent the area from becoming muddy and allow for easy cleaning using a hose.

Food and water

You will be feeding your birds every day, so plan feed storage to be as close to their accommodation as possible. Ideally you should have a water source near the house or be within easy reach of a hose, for topping up and cleaning water containers as well as washing off hardstanding.

Take a seat

Finally, you will want to spend time enjoying your birds, so position a garden seat nearby where you can sit and watch their antics, and get to know them.

Choosing a house

Ducks and geese have simple needs, but there can be serious consequences if these are not met. For their housing, good ventilation, dryness, security from predators, and sufficient space are the absolute basics.

You will need a house even if you have a large pond with an island – the theory that the birds can sleep safely on the island is quite simply wrong, because some predators can and do swim. Not only that, but the birds will rise with the sun in the quiet of the early morning and swim straight into the jaws of waiting predators.

Size

The number of ducks or geese you can keep in a particular house depends on the size of the breed. As a rough guide, you will need about 4 sq ft (0.4 sq m) per bird for the larger ducks and a minimum of 7 sq ft (0.6 sq m) per goose – more if they are shut in for any longer than the night-time period.

   Although the birds will roost on the ground, the house needs some height to allow for air flow: around 3 ft (1 m) for ducks and 5 ft (1.5 m) upwards for geese.

Purpose-built house

There are many excellent examples of purpose-built duck sheds on the market. For smaller numbers of ducks, they are nearly all movable. Unlike chickens, ducks are not agile and will need ramps if the house is to be raised off the ground, so check if these are included. For both ducks and geese, the door to the house must be wide enough for more than one bird to pass through at a time, otherwise the competition to get through it will be very uncomfortable for them. Geese are large birds and need a good-sized door that allows them to pass through without ducking or

catching themselves on the sides. A chicken pophole should not be used for either species.

Shed or barn

If you have an old garden shed or perhaps a small barn or stable, there is no reason why you cannot adapt it for your birds. Old sheds that have housed poultry can be infected with parasites, such as red mites, or even disease, and should be cleaned thoroughly. If the building is made from wood, check carefully that it is absolutely sound: predators, such as

Above Small, moveable duck/chicken ark for nighttime only or with a run. The perches inside need to be taken out for ducks.

rats, foxes, badgers, coyotes, or racoons, will find a way into any construction that is even slightly flimsy. A new garden shed can also be adapted – remove the glass or plastic from the windows and replace it with mesh to facilitate ventilation.

Construction

If you are building a shed, position the windows high up so that air enters from the top rather than sweeping across the sleeping birds. This also makes it more difficult for predators to look in at the birds.

The roof should keep the house dry and drain water away efficiently, which may mean adding guttering. The floor should be dry. In very well-drained, dry areas, you might be able to place the house straight on to the ground on top of wire mesh (kept well covered with litter so the birds don't hurt their feet), but in most situations you will need dry slabs or concrete as a base, preferably with a very slight slope for drainage.

Housing checklist

✔ Waterfowl will not do well in a stuffy, damp house.

✔ The house must be strong enough to keep your birds in, and determined predators out.

✔ Make sure your birds have enough space.

✔ Doors must be adequately wide.

✔ Clean secondhand housing thoroughly and treat wooden sheds with preservatives.

Wood must be strong and purpose-made buildings are almost always treated with preservatives. If you treat an old building, make sure you keep the birds out of it for the specified time as fresh preservatives can be

Above A strongly built duck house with a good-sized door.

Above Housing should be well ventilated and dry.

harmful to them. Each chemical is different, so read the instructions carefully before use. It's best to treat the outside of the house every year.

Nesting and laying

Inside, the house should be well ventilated and dry. Unlike hens, ducks do not use nestboxes and could not climb into them anyway, nor do they need perches. They like to lay their eggs in a nest and will make this themselves in a secluded part of the house when

Above Ornamental waterfowl need a range of housing. This is a tree duck house with ramp.

provided with sufficient litter. You can try setting aside an area for laying, but the birds will often choose their own spot or simply lay anywhere. The floor litter must therefore be kept clean or it will soil the eggs. Collect eggs at least once a day, plus whenever you see them.

You can create a special nest area for a goose or simply provide sufficient litter and she will make her own. For more details for both ducks and geese, see pages 54–57.

Cleaning

As you will have to keep the bird house clean, it is best if it is big enough for you to be able to get inside it comfortably in order to do so. As ducks and geese are quite messy, it is essential that you are able to clean their house easily and frequently.

Companions

Ideally, ducks should live separately to poultry but in a big enough space they will co-exist, with the poultry perching and the ducks on the floor. Hens make less mess than ducks and of course are not as wet, so you will have to be careful the house does not become too damp for them. Geese should not be housed with poultry.

Housing other waterfowl

Ornamental and wildfowl have different housing needs than domestic ducks and geese. They require a large, aviary-type structure to keep them confined as they can and do fly, unless they have had their wings clipped or pinioned (see page 194). There are many different species from different habitats, and ducks in particular display varied behaviors: some are diving ducks, some tree ducks, some like to go underground, and some into tunnels or bushes. Before planning their housing, you need to understand your breed's natural habitat and behaviors, and construct their enclosure accordingly. For more details, see pages 194–197.

Getting Started

Fencing

If you are fencing solely to keep your birds in, 3 ft (1 m) high will be adequate. You can use any type of wood and/or wire construction that prevents the birds getting through gaps. Fencing predators out is a different matter. The barrier will need to be at least 6 ft (2 m) high and the top must be electrified or have an overhang so that predators cannot climb over. Hunters can also dig, so you may have to sink the fence into the ground or run an electric wire along the bottom (make sure it does not touch the ground or it will charge the earth). It is worth getting it erected professionally, as it needs to be well strained and there should be no gaps between the gate and gateposts or the fence and ground through which predators could enter.

Electric poultry netting can be effective, especially for daytime-only protection, but it needs to be well erected and certainly not floppy. In addition, ducks and geese do seem to take a while to realize that it is electrified, so they may put their heads through it and be hurt or killed by the current.

Any electric fence is only as good as its current: if you are relying on it to keep out predators it must work all the time. A fence tester is a useful and inexpensive piece of equipment that will tell you if the fence is operational. You will need to make sure that the fencing unit is efficient, the fence is not grounding or shorting anywhere, and that you have two batteries, one on the fence and one charging. Solar fence chargers are also available. Alternatively, you can run a fence from the mains. If it is in a public place, you will need to fix a warning notice to it regardless of whether it is run from the mains or a battery.

Water

"Like a duck to water," "Goslings lead geese to water": these two old proverbs emphasize the crucial importance of water to waterfowl. However, not all types require the same expanse, so you will need to understand your birds' preferences.

Natural behaviors

All waterfowl need some sort of clean water available at all times, but how much depends entirely on the breed and their natural behavior. Dabbling and diving ducks will need access to fairly deep water, but most domestic ducks and geese do not fall into this category.

Many breeds, especially geese, manage very well with a large bucket in which they are able to submerge their heads and thereby clean their eyes and nostrils. Without this facility, their eyes and beaks would soon become sticky, the birds miserable, and eventually they might even develop disease.

Above Ducks and geese must be able to submerge their heads and necks in water.

Above A tub in which the water can be refreshed regularly, for geese.

Above Splashing water for preening is essential.

All ducks and geese also need splashing water to throw over their feathers. Waterfowl have a preen gland located on the lower rump near the tail. This is activated when the birds splash water over themselves, rubbing their heads and necks over it. The gland then releases the preening oil essential for a duck or goose to keep its plumage in good order. Lack of oil will cause the bird to become waterlogged as the water cannot run off, and it may even drown. In addition, covering themselves in water, wing beating, splashing, and preening are all part of the natural behaviors of a waterbird which it must be able to carry out in order to stay healthy and content, and to prepare for mating.

Portable pools

Domestic ducks and geese generally manage very well with a small pond such as a child's rigid paddling pool, large plastic bowl (more than one if you have several birds), purpose-made duck pond or rubber tub. The water must be plentiful and clean – ducks and geese will foul small areas of water very quickly indeed

Safety warning

It doesn't take much depth of water at all for a child to drown, so keep young children away from the waterfowl pond or stream at all times. As well as the risk of drowning, the water may have become foul so if anyone, of any age, is immersed in it they should wash thoroughly and change their clothes. Occasional visitors to your premises should be warned that children should be supervised at all times.

and the great advantage of all these small pools is that they are so easy to clean. Bear in mind that the area around the container will become very wet and muddy if on soil, so move it from time to time and/or site it somewhere that drains well. In the summer you will need to put out some more containers or fill them up more frequently.

Above Natural water on your property always provides much enjoyment for waterfowl.

Domestic ducks will need some help to get into the water, so provide a ramp that is stable enough to take them. Geese should generally be able to manage without. Don't forget that the birds need to be able to get out of the pool as well – a strategically positioned brick or block will help. In winter, when it is wetter, both ducks and geese really enjoy splashing around in puddles, so if possible leave a few areas where they can form, purely for the birds' enjoyment.

Permanent ponds

An artificial pond, usually constructed from concrete, is another option. Concrete is preferable to simply sinking a polythene liner into the ground because this can be torn by duck breeds that have sharp claws. A really heavy-duty liner may be satisfactory, provided it is laid correctly and – as with any pond for waterfowl – not overstocked with birds.

Both types of pond must be cleaned out from time to time, so should be built with a slope down to a drain for easy emptying. The sides of the pond should slope gently so that the birds can get in and out easily. The area around the pond will become fouled and very muddy, so it is a good idea to use smooth gravel that will drain or some kind of hard surface that can be cleaned.

Natural water

The idea of keeping waterfowl may have come from already having a stream, river, or natural pond on your land. One advantage of all types of natural water is that the birds will happily get much of their nourishment from plants growing in and around it. Duckweed in particular is greatly enjoyed.

Stream or river

The ideal area of natural water is one that flows, so that the water is always clean. To contain the birds you can erect a fence across the stream – if you want to keep more than one breed, subdivide the stream so that each has its own section and they cannot mingle and interbreed. It is also possible to semi-dam or divert a stream to form ponds, but in many areas you will need permission and even a licence from the appropriate authorities to do so. As with all waterfowl keeping, the key is not to overstock any one area.

Even with free-flowing water, the birds will add their excrement to it so you will need to look out for it becoming foul. You will also need to deal with water-based predators such as mink if they are present in your area (see pages 38–39). Remember, too, that at certain times of the year even a gentle stream can turn into a deluge, break over your fence, and quite literally wash the birds downstream.

It is a good idea to get the water tested initially, especially if you are unsure of its origins; you will need to check whether it is polluted in any way before you put in the birds. Equally, you should ensure that your birds will not be polluting a stream that flows into a neighbor's property.

Pond or lake

If you are lucky enough to have a large pond or small lake, this will greatly extend the range of waterfowl you can keep. The usual checks apply: the birds must be kept safe from predators, confined to the area and shut in at night. Fortunately, ducks and geese will learn to

Water checklist

- ✔ Ducks and geese must be provided with water for washing and preening.
- ✔ Some breeds benefit more from access to water than others.
- ✔ Portable tubs and pools can fulfil the requirements of many breeds.
- ✔ Water should be kept clean, so construct ponds that can be emptied.
- ✔ Use existing water for maximum benefit.
- ✔ Beware of wild water-based predators and take steps to protect your birds against them (see pages 38–39).
- ✔ Be safe – young children can drown in very shallow water.

come off the water and into their house by use of feed at the appropriate time.

A pond or lake with waterfowl will need attention and maintenance – you will need to ensure that plants are not being destroyed, the water does not become foul, and that the banks remain accessible to the birds. You may want to make two or more little shores so that the birds do not congregate in just one area.

There is debate as to whether waterfowl will destroy other aquatic life such as fish and amphibians. However, it is clear that the fewer birds you have in a given area, the greater the chance that plants and other water life will co-exist with the waterfowl, as indeed they do in nature.

Although many breeds can live quite well with only water to splash in and submerge their heads, their joy at being able to swim, even in a comparatively small pond, is well worth the effort required to provide one.

Safe and secure

It is your responsibility to keep your waterfowl safe from predators. These come in many forms: winged, four-legged, and sometimes two-legged! You will need to take all the precautions you can to protect your birds from harm by such outside agencies.

Who are the predators?

Ducks, and even imposing geese, suffer from having many predators that want to both harm and eat them.

Top of the list is the fox. You may never have seen one in your area, but you can be sure that as soon as you get your waterfowl home they will appear, unable to resist the lure of the birds. The rat population will also increase, tempted by additional feed.

Depending on where you live, there are plenty of other would-be diners including weasels, stoats, bobcats, polecats, racoons, and mink, although the

Above Foxes seem to come from nowhere when you keep waterfowl.

latter generally only live near natural water. Winged predators such as hawks, owls, crows, jays, and magpies are capable of taking very small birds such as ducklings or goslings. Many predators – birds in particular, but also badgers – are very attracted to eggs, so make doubly sure the bird house is secure.

Some areas are worse for predators than others: for example, if your garden adjoins a wood you might expect more problems than if you live in open country where there are no hiding places.

Protecting your birds

As it is both impractical and undesirable to wipe out all of nature in order to keep your waterfowl safe, it follows that you will need to fence securely and shut the birds in a predator-proof house at night to keep them safe (see pages 30–33 and 42–43). It is also comparatively easy to protect ducklings and goslings from bigger birds by penning them until they are a reasonable size. Protection for the birds rather than destruction of the predator is the key.

However, there are some predators you will need to control. If you see one rat, you can be sure there is another close by and possibly under the ground. A rat has quite a large territory and you will need to control the numbers. There are several methods including shooting, trapping, and poisoning. All must be carried out responsibly, with the least amount of suffering.

• Shooting must only be carried by an experienced person who holds the appropriate licences and can kill the animal outright without causing danger to people or other animals.

- If you choose to trap, you must check the traps every day and have a plan as to how you are going to dispose of the live rat. If the trap is designed to kill the rat, check that it has done so – if not, do not leave the animal to suffer.
- Poisons have become faster-acting and more reliable, but the bait must be set safely away from domestic animals and children, and the resulting corpses cleared quickly before they can be eaten by another animal.
- Drowning is *not* an option as it is slow and extremely cruel.
- Mink are increasingly common and you will have to call in an expert to dispose of them.

Foxes are more difficult to eradicate, and if you remove one then another is likely to move into the territory and begin the whole cycle again. Most country foxes are shy and you won't see them during the day unless it is exceptionally quiet or they are particularly hungry. It is the semi-tame urban foxes that are the bigger problem, as they have no fear and will take birds during the day, sometimes right in front of you. As with rats, if you use a live trap then you must have a plan for immediate and humane disposal, and if you shoot then you must be able to kill the animal outright.

Domestic danger

Waterfowl may also be attacked by domestic dogs, which can sometimes return to kill again and again. As well as protecting your stock, you will also need to seek out the owner and, if necessary, take legal advice. You must train your own dog from the beginning not to touch the birds, or keep him away from them unless he is on a leash. Do not allow friends or family members to let their dogs loose unless you are absolutely certain they are well behaved.

Escaped ferrets, too, can do a huge amount of damage in a very short time. You will need to catch the offender and return it to its owner or take it to an animal shelter.

Above If you see a single rat you can be sure that there will be many more nearby.

Domestic cats are not a threat to fully grown birds, and ducklings and goslings should already be well protected from all predators anyway. Your family cat will keep other cats away, as will your dog. Your own dog is good protection not only against other dogs but also against foxes and other predators, which do not normally like to explore where there is a loose dog, although with semi-tame foxes this may not always be the case.

Two-legged predators

Unfortunately, some of your fellow human beings are not above stealing ducks and geese, especially at festival times such as Christmas or if they are rare breeds. Keep your birds safe and secure, and away from prying eyes. Always report mysterious disappearances to the police rather than assuming the culprit is an animal predator. Contact veterinary surgeons and local animal shelters with a description – sometimes a fright can make them wander.

Care and Attention

Your birds depend on you for all their needs including food, water and security, freedom from bullying by others, and treatment if they are sick. Although this is a big responsibility which you will need to take seriously, it is also a rewarding one.

Everyday care

Daily care is the commitment you have to make to your ducks and geese. It need not be simply a chore: it is a great opportunity to interact with your birds and watch their enjoyment of the things you provide.

Care and Attention

Daily routine

A good design of house and run (see pages 28–33) will help to make daily life easier for you and your birds. Although ducks and geese need regular, routine attention, on most days it won't take up a lot of time.

In the morning, let your birds out into the run or free range, depending on which system you have chosen.

Check that they have plenty of clean water, especially if you are about to leave for work and won't be returning for several hours. Provide sufficient food for health and to prevent boredom, in suitable containers (see pages 22–23) so that the food won't get trodden into the ground. Collect any eggs – if you let the birds out very early you will need to check again later, as ducks and

Left Man-made, shallow ponds need emptying and cleaning on a regular basis.

geese tend to lay during the morning. If you use electric fencing, check that it is working (see page 33).

In the evening, the routine is reversed: make a final check for eggs and then shut the birds in their house for the night. Water and food are not necessary during the hours of darkness, but if possible it is a good idea to remove any feed bowls containing uneaten food. A metal bin or box that is impregnable to vermin can be placed next to the run and the containers placed inside for the night. This deters rodents, which would otherwise cost you money by eating the food and can also be destructive and possibly dangerous to you and the birds. An automatic feeder will also help to reduce vermin (see pages 22–23). Do not overfeed your birds: if they are regularly leaving large amounts of feed, then you are giving too much or there is something wrong with the feed.

Observing your waterfowl

Perhaps the most important daily routine care of all is your observation. As someone new to keeping waterfowl, train yourself to gather information on your birds' health and happiness by answering the following questions:

- Are all the birds coming eagerly out of the house? Count them if necessary.
- If they are in a run, glance along the fence line. Are there any vermin holes or have the birds made a gap under the fence?
- Is the house unpleasantly warm when you let them out? If you find it warm, the birds will be very hot.
- How much food have they eaten? Are you feeding too much, too little, or do they not like the food?
- Is there plenty of water for the day ahead? They may need an extra container in hot weather.
- What is the weather today? If it is very wet, do you need to add more bedding? If very hot, do you need to provide more shade?
- How many eggs are they laying?

- Are any of the birds being bullied, or bullying the others?
- Are any males causing distress to the females?
- Are any of the birds limping?
- Is the birds' plumage clean or dirty? Perhaps they need more washing water or the males are being over-amorous.
- Is *anything* different to normal?

If you are not happy with the answer to any of these questions, you can then take immediate steps to put it right. This is what makes a good stock person for any species of bird or animal: the ability to notice something different and take action before the situation develops.

Take time to be with your birds whenever you can, to watch their behavior and get to know them as individuals. They do have different personalities: some are pushy, some are timid, some are adventurous.

Above Check that the birds are alert and keen to leave the house.

Note their place within the flock: is a particular bird a leader or a follower? If you know how your birds behave normally, it is easier to recognize – and interpret – unusual behavior. And of course, it's also relaxing for you to spend time interacting with your birds.

Record keeping

This goes hand in hand with observation. Your records need not be detailed or complicated, but can simply be notes made on your calendar (although if you want to keep a special notebook you'll find it very helpful for the future). At the very least, keep a note of how many eggs you are collecting on a daily basis and the weather conditions. Other notes such as "White Call duck slightly lame" will remind you to keep an eye on the situation; if it deteriorates, you will be able to check exactly how long the bird has been unwell. "New bag of duck food" will help you to monitor how much you are feeding.

If you have to get someone else to look after your birds for a few days, your notes will be invaluable in giving them a picture of the flock. Over the years you may see patterns emerging as problems often occur at the same time each year, so you can then anticipate and deal with these before they happen.

Weekly tasks

Ducks and geese are very messy creatures, producing quantities of loose droppings and fouling their water. You will have emptied water containers on a daily basis, but at least once a week you will need to empty out shallow man-made ponds and hose them clean (see pages 34–37). You'll also need to clean out the bird house, sweep (and possibly hose) any hard surfaces free of droppings, and rake the run. The size and design of the house and run will determine just how easy or difficult these tasks are.

Buy yourself some good tools: you're going to be

Working among your birds

Always move quietly when you are with your birds, however urgent the task in which you are engaged. Don't allow other people to be loud around them either; keep all but the very best behaved dogs away – you may find the birds are upset by even a docile dog – and never, ever allow children to scream at or chase after them. Waterfowl are peaceful creatures and quite easily become very agitated. Their instincts have prepared them to be ready for flight if surprised by any danger, real or perceived – the alternative in the wild is probably to be caught and eaten. If you always work quietly around them, your birds will come to know you and appreciate your efforts and not become alarmed.

using them a lot. A big, heavy-duty broom, while excellent for sweeping larger yards, may be just too cumbersome for working in your bird house and run, so it is better to choose a smaller, lighter version. You will need a flexible rake, a shovel (again, not too large), and a three- or four-pronged pitchfork. Other useful items include a paint scraper to remove dried-on droppings and a hand brush.

Whatever floor covering you use – shavings, straw or some other suitable material – it will need to be kept clean. Make sure you have sufficient supplies to hand so that the house never becomes really wet. If the run and house are always very badly soiled, you are keeping too many birds in too small a space.

Check all fencing thoroughly for weak spots or gaps, and make sure electric fences are functioning. For geese, check around the grass area on which

Left Work quietly around your birds and they will not be alarmed.

45

Care and Attention

they roam for any dangers such as wire, glass, or plastic that has blown in. Note how much grass they have eaten and if there is sufficient remainings, or whether some areas are becoming muddy and may be permanently damaged.

As with any hobby, duck and goose keeping is an interest that continues to grow and although you may not notice it, your daily observations will build into a real picture of how ducks and geese behave, their breeding cycles, and their nutritional needs. You may well wish to change or modify your original plans for housing, to construct small or even larger ponds or seek out waterfowl friendly plants. Far from being a chore, daily and weekly care of your birds is something that will be rewarding and a constant interest.

Handling and traveling

It is important to learn how to handle your birds correctly as this will make life more pleasant for all of you. You will need and/or want to handle some waterfowl more than others, depending on the breed and the circumstances.

A calm environment

When your birds first arrive, they won't know you and you won't know them. As you start to work with them, feeding them every day and getting in among them, they will gradually become more used to you. Adult birds may well remain wary all their life, but even if they don't become really tame they will still relate to you and eventually be able to pick you out from other people.

You need to be quiet around your birds at all times and insist that anyone with you does the same

(see pages 44–45). That doesn't mean not speaking: you can talk to your birds all the time in a quiet, even voice but never scream or shout. If you feel annoyed for whatever reason, walk away. The birds won't understand your anger and will simply become fearful.

Waterfowl and other pets

Keep all potentially threatening animals, such as dogs, away from your birds (see pages 38–39). They will become used to a well-mannered dog,

Right Think safety when geese share with grazing animals.

Left A pet carrier, if large enough, is suitable for traveling ducks.

47

Care and Attention

but not to one that is barking and playing with them – the birds will see this as threatening behavior.

It is a rare family cat that is a threat to ducks – most cats don't want to take on even the smaller Call ducks (they are too noisy!), although ducklings can be a different matter. Conversely, large birds such as the bigger geese can do damage to cats, and even dogs, if they feel threatened or are protecting a mate or young. To be on the safe side, keep vulnerable pets such as an elderly cat or very small dog away from large adult geese.

If geese are sharing a paddock with grazing animals you will need to ensure that there is harmony. Unfortunately, geese and ducks can be trampled by larger animals such as horses and may not be quick enough to get out of the way, although many share paddocks quite happily. For example, old horses and ponies may be quite calm about sharing their field with ducks and geese, but a paddock full of flighty youngsters can be a different matter.

Catching

When you need to catch one of your birds, time spent planning is never wasted. The scenario to be avoided at all costs is aimless chasing and grabbing at the bird.

It's best to catch a duck or goose at dusk as it is going to roost. If this is not an option – perhaps you want to examine an off-color bird or check the flock for parasites in daylight – then you should plan your approach carefully. You could leave the birds shut in their house and carry out the handling before letting them out, or perhaps drive them gently into another confined space and then catch them. If you have hurdles or fencing to hand, you can position these as a "tunnel" to walk the birds through and into a catching area. A funnel design, wider at the top and narrowing to the catching pen, is usually the most effective.

Once you have your birds confined, keep still and let them settle. There is no point in trying to grab at birds that are flapping in every direction. Gently edge closer and, when appropriate, make your move, confidently and decisively. Your next task is to get control of the wings as they can so easily be damaged – and a large bird's wings can do you some damage in return. Grasp them gently but firmly to keep them still.

If you fail to catch the bird after two or three attempts, leave it and go back to the planning stages. Repeated attempts that fail will unnerve the bird and make things even worse as you continue.

Ducks

When you have caught the bird and restrained the wings, bring it towards your body. Keeping the wings restrained, slide your hand under the body and gently catch the legs between your fingers. Do not pull the legs close together as you could damage the bird internally – keep at least two fingers between the legs.

Above Always restrain the wings of a goose – watch out for the beak as well.

Never, ever carry a bird upside down by its legs: there is never a time when it is acceptable to do this and it will cause both distress and damage to the bird.

You should end up with one hand under the bird gently grasping the legs and the other hand on top, holding the bird against your body and preventing the wings from flapping. The hand and arm under the bird will support its weight. The head and neck will be either under your arm or against it. In this position you can hold even a lively bird quite securely and comfortably for both of you. Practice on a docile bird, ideally under the supervision of someone who is used to handling ducks.

Geese

You need to realize that these birds are very strong and they can do you damage. First grasp the bird securely by the neck or wings to bring it towards you. When carrying, support the weight and hold the bird in the same way as for a duck. It's best to cover any bare flesh as a goose's beak can give you a painful nip, and make sure it doesn't get near your lips or nose – keep the bird's head away from your head unless you know it to be tame and docile.

To reiterate: do not underestimate a goose's size and strength. You need to be confident in handling these large birds. By now you will have realized how important it is for your geese to be tame, and you should make every effort to keep your flock as calm as possible. How far you can go with this will depend on the age at which you got them and their natural temperament and breed. If they arrived as goslings you have every chance of producing a tame and trusting goose through frequent, gentle handling, hand feeding and plenty of contact.

Traveling with your birds

As with catching, traveling with your birds requires planning. Special carry boxes are available for

Above A duck correctly held and therefore comfortable.

ducks and geese but are relatively expensive so are probably not an option unless you are showing regularly. A strong cardboard box makes an adequate substitute, but remember that cardboard is warm and waterfowl need cool conditions. They will overheat quickly, so you need to travel in the cooler times of the day and ensure that the box is well provided with air holes – not so big that the birds can get their heads out or escape, but large enough to allow a good flow of air. It is better to box geese individually as two birds create more heat than one. If necessary, travel with the car windows open or air conditioning switched on. Try not to make lengthy journeys and if you do, don't make them any longer or more uncomfortable by stopping and leaving the birds in the vehicle with the windows closed.

Travel checklist

✔ **Keep birds cool in transit.**

✔ **Boxes should be large enough to allow birds to stand, but not so large that they move around excessively and lack support.**

✔ **Make sure you obey local animal transport regulations.**

✔ **Drive with care – avoid sudden movements.**

For ducks, a pet carrier – especially the covered-wire variety – is suitable. Poultry crates are well ventilated and strong but too small for the larger breeds. A Runner duck needs to be able to stand up and stretch its neck, so for this breed you may need a suitable cardboard box or larger pet carrier.

Carriers must be easy to clean: cardboard has the advantage that it can be discarded (or recycled). Make sure that the cardboard is thick enough that the bottom doesn't drop out of the box as you carry it – add extra layers of cardboard inside the base if necessary and wood shavings to absorb liquid.

There's no need to give food and water on short journeys, but longer ones will require more planning. Many countries have animal transport regulations that apply to poultry and must be followed, so check before you travel.

Commonsense dictates that you shouldn't stack cardboard boxes on top of each other in case they collapse, and that you never shut birds in the car's trunk where they will certainly suffer and probably suffocate or die from heatstroke. Make sure that the boxes can't move around, and when driving be careful not to stop quickly or make jerky moves as the birds will lose their footing in their boxes. Try to make their ride as pleasant as possible.

Feeding

Feeding your ducks and geese correctly will help to ensure they remain healthy and live comfortably to a good age. Follow the simple guidelines given here to make sure your birds receive the most suitable nutrition for their type and age.

First considerations

A domestic duck or goose depends entirely on you for its well-being. Feeding is especially important, as the bird only has access to whatever land you choose to give it and the feedstuffs you select. Feeding ducks and geese is relatively simple but you will need to ask yourself the following questions before making your final decision.

- How free range are your birds?
- What age are they?
- What is their breed or type?
- What do you want them to be – layers, table birds, exhibition standard birds, pets?
- What have they been fed on up to now?

Feed containers

All feeds should be placed in open containers that cannot be overturned. You will need sufficient containers to hold enough feed for all the birds (see pages 22–23). If you don't have enough containers for them all to feed comfortably, then the greedy ones will eat their fill and the timid ones will get whatever (if anything) is left. Feed left in containers quickly deteriorates in quality and becomes putrid. If your feeders are remaining full, it may be that you are feeding too much and the excess has become stale and possibly moldy, so no longer appeals to the birds. Remove all uneaten food at least once a week.

A balanced diet

A bird will require a mixture of vitamins, minerals, protein, oil, and fiber in varying amounts according to whether it is breeding, laying eggs, growing, or an adult.

If your flock has sufficient free range the birds may be able to balance their own diet to some extent, depending on what is available. If they are more confined, then providing the correct proportion of the various nutrients in their feed ration becomes more important. Compound, bagged feeds are available that cater for each type and time of a bird's life. They can be pelleted or, for ducks, mashed (creating a dry, powdery substance). It is essential to mix this mash with water before giving it to ducks (unlike chickens, which can be fed dry to help prevent feather pecking). Most duck keepers choose pellets.

These days bagged feed does not contain meat protein. It may or may not be GM-free or organic, but this will be declared on the bag. If the feed is organic,

Above Wildfowl pellets, domestic waterfowl pellets, and mixed grains.

Feeding checklist

✔ Ducks and geese need water by their feed – they are waterbirds! If they eat dry pellets or food and then drink later, the food could swell up and cause discomfort or even death.

✔ Even if the birds you have acquired were not eating a balanced diet, make changes to it gradually until it is the ration you feel is right for them. Sudden, wholesale changes to the diet can upset the birds' digestion.

✔ Remove anything that might be dangerous – such as large quantities of white bread – from the diet straightaway.

Grower pellets These follow on from the starter ration from around four to six weeks old.

Finisher pellets These are used for the final stage of fattening a table bird. For geese, this will be from late summer until slaughter, and for ducks the last two weeks before slaughter.

Breeder pellets If you want the best chance of your stock successfully raising young, feed these during the breeding season.

General/pet pellets These are for maintenance, for pet birds and for those not breeding or laying.

Layer pellets These are designed to support a duck in lay and are an essential part of the diet for a bird that is producing eggs, especially a high-laying duck. They contain additional calcium, which is needed for the bird to be able to produce the eggshell without detriment to her own body.

Ornamental waterfowl pellets These are designed for ornamental rather than domestic waterfowl (see pages 194–197). Such birds can include species that source some of their diet from insect larvae and small shellfish and therefore require specialist mixes.

Although ideally you should try to buy waterfowl or specialist duck or goose rations, for many years

the certifying body will be shown on the bag. The type of feed and exact balance of the ration should also be shown clearly, for example: 15% protein, 3% oil, 8% fiber, and then a list of the vitamins and minerals.

The most important thing to check on the label is the freshness date. Feeding after that date may do no harm, but there is a risk that the feed could be getting stale and, more likely, that the vitamins and minerals are losing their effectiveness.

Compound feeds

Starter crumbs These are essential for ducklings or goslings from hatching. They have a high protein level as birds grow quickly at this age. Chicken starter crumbs are not ideal for waterfowl, which need to consume more niacin than chickens. In addition, chicken starter crumbs usually include a coccidiostat which can be harmful to ducklings and goslings. If you have to use them, check that they are coccidiostat free. Choose a duck or goose starter crumb if at all possible.

Above Evaluate how much the birds are getting from free ranging.

waterfowl keepers had to buy hen laying pellets as no other type was available. If you do this, it is best to buy free-range layer pellets as they contain fewer additives, which means less chance of there being something unsuitable for waterfowl. Avoid commercial pellets for intensive chicken layers, broiler feeds for chickens, and turkey pellets of all kinds – these often contain additives or are very high in protein, which will cause a problem for waterfowl.

Grain feeds

Ducks love grain and, in particular, whole wheat. Wheat contains an average of 10 percent protein, some less and the breadmaking wheats considerably more. It all depends on the source. Maize, fed kibbled or cracked rather than whole, is better fed

(with wheat grains) in the winter as it contains more carbohydrate and fat.

If ducks do not have access to any free-range feed, wheat on its own will not provide all the nutrients they need. For this reason it is best to feed it in the afternoon, as it will be eaten in preference to the balanced ration that you want them to consume. Provide this first thing in the morning when the ducks are hungry. Grain can be fed in water as well.

Geese will also enjoy a little grain as a supplement to their grazing.

Ducks on range and in water

If you have your ducks on a stream, lake, or part of a river, they will be finding a good proportion of their food for themselves. Similarly, ducks on range in a

Above Ducks feeding from an open container that cannot be overturned.

Above Grass for grazing geese needs to be well-maintained.

pasture, orchard, or garden will be kept constantly busy finding food, ranging from grubs to foliage. They really enjoy doing this – your job is then simply to provide supplementary feeding to achieve a good, balanced diet. You can also feed your ducks cold, boiled potatoes and soaked bread. Opinions differ as to whether bread can be harmful, but small amounts that are thoroughly soaked appear to do no harm. Make absolutely certain that the bread has no mold on it. Some ducks also enjoy cabbage, cucumber, and lettuce.

Geese on grass

To begin with, geese will need both starter crumbs and grower pellets but by the time they are around two months old grass should be providing much of their ration. Depending on how well grown the birds are, by four months or so they should be able to manage largely on grass with maybe a supplement of grain. Obviously the grass needs to be fresh, plentiful, and of good nutritional value; by late summer the nutrients in the grass will have declined, so grain and possibly a bagged feed will then be essential. If you are fattening your birds, you will need to increase the ration considerably in order for them to put on weight for the table.

As grass is a major contribution to your geese's diet, you need to look after it. Keep it clean, shut off parts in rotation to let it regrow and to keep it fresh, and reseed if necessary. If your grass is poor or has been eaten down, you will have to increase the quantity of supplementary feed and also provide some additional green matter, such as vegetable waste for the birds.

Grit

Inside a bird's beak you will not find any teeth, yet they still have to grind up their food. This is done by means of a gizzard, in which the food is ground down. To function, the gizzard needs grit.

If your birds have access to a reasonable range they will probably find their own grit, but it is advisable to supply some anyway. If they are more confined, it is essential. Mixed poultry grit is the usual choice – you need to ensure it is in insoluble form so that it does not dissolve in water. If your birds are laying, you will also need soluble grit such as oystershell to help provide calcium for the eggshells. You can keep and crush the duck or goose eggshells and add that to the grit as well. Wash them first but only in plain water, without detergent.

How much to feed?

The amount of feed an individual duck or goose will eat depends on its size, age (young birds eat a lot more), and the stage of its life (breeding or laying). As a rough guide to help you estimate how much feed you might need to buy, you can expect a medium-sized duck to eat 4–6 oz (120–180 g) per day. You will need to work out for yourself how much to give each day: the birds should finish all the feed or leave just a little, but they need to be satisfied. Don't overfeed, because waste food must be thrown away, and don't underfeed, especially if you have purchased a duck that lays a high number of eggs.

Eggs

Some breeds of duck lay large numbers of eggs, and if you are not breeding from your geese you may find yourself with some goose eggs, too. Both eggs are attractive to look at and have their own special uses.

Duck eggs

A duck egg weighs around 2½–3 oz (80–95 g), in comparison to a hen's egg which weighs up to around 2¼ oz (70 g) for a very large egg. Usually white, they can also be greenish, or even dark or bluish green.

Duck eggs have a higher fat content than hen's eggs. This makes them perfect for baking and they do taste a little richer. Be patient when you cook a duck egg: a thoroughly hardboiled egg will take over ten minutes to cook through.

Goose eggs

A goose egg is seriously large, weighing in at 6–6½ oz (180–200 g). The shells are very hard

Above A normal hen's egg shows the large size of goose eggs.

and white. An individual egg can make a sizeable omelette: other uses include baking and perhaps hardboiling, then slicing into a salad. However, their popular use is in egg painting and decorating, which is a popular pastime. Once local craft enthusiasts know you have geese that lay, they will want to purchase your eggs. If you don't want to sell them within a time constraint after laying, learn how to blow them – that is, remove their contents. Traditionally, a larger hole is pierced at the thick end and a smaller one at the pointy end. Break the contents by inserting a small pin and then simply blow them out. Wash the egg and leave it to dry. The eggshells are, of course, very fragile and should be packed away carefully until sold.

Breed and feed

If you want to get eggs from your birds, there are two factors to consider. First is the choice of bird. Khaki Campbell or Indian Runner ducks are very good layers, with the Campbell sometimes producing more eggs than a free range hen – 250 plus per year is not uncommon. For geese, the Chinese variety lay a higher number of smaller eggs. A flock of commercial geese that are reared for the table might average around 60 eggs in their first year of laying, but for many breeds 20 or so is the norm.

The second factor is feeding. You will get more eggs from low-laying strains if you feed for laying; conversely you will reduce the number of eggs that are produced by high-laying breeds if you don't feed enough nutrients.

Left Chinese geese lay more but smaller eggs than other breeds.

55

Care and Attention

Laying patterns

A duck will come into lay at 21–27 weeks old, perhaps later if the weather is particularly poor. It used to be said that "a duck will not lay until it has tasted Lide (March) water," partly because in the absence of compound feeds spring growth and insects were required to make up the protein needed for laying. Now, in order to lay 300 plus eggs per year, high-laying breeds developed in the mid-twentieth century lay more or less all year round except when in molt. They will continue to lay well for up to four years, although some quite elderly ducks can still produce respectable numbers of eggs.

Geese usually come into lay when the days begin to lengthen in late winter/early spring and generally stop laying in early to midsummer. A goose will continue to lay for many years, although after the age of six egg numbers will decline.

Laying an egg

A bird's ovary is activated by increasing day length. Ovulation occurs when one of the minute egg cells already in place in the bird's body starts to enlarge and becomes an ovarian follicle. This is then released into the oviduct, where fertilization (if it occurs) takes place. The egg continues to develop

Left It's great collecting eggs
and the whole family can help!

through the isthmus and into the uterine section of
the oviduct, where the shell is formed. Finally, just
before it is laid, a secretion from the vagina covers
the egg to seal it against germs. Egg laying takes just
a few minutes.

From ovulation to egg laying takes about 24 hours.
That's why if you purchase laying ducks they will often
lay on the first day – because the egg is already in
the process of forming and cannot reverse – but then
won't lay for a few more days until they have adapted
to their new surroundings. The process of egg
development highlights another reason why careful
handling is so important, because if you crush the
egg in the oviduct you can cause the bird's death
by egg peritonitis.

As the duck or goose keeper, your job in all of
this is to provide optimum conditions for the bird to
develop her egg. Correct feeding is vital, and she also
needs plenty of water as a high proportion of an egg
is liquid.

Where to lay?

The bird now needs somewhere to lay her egg. A duck is comparatively easy to satisfy – she will even lay on her way to the pond. Try putting a low edge that she can easily step over – such as a plank of wood about 6 in (15 cm) deep – against the furthest wall inside the house and fill it with straw. Place pot (ceramic) eggs in the area where you want her to lay. Don't let her out really early, as ducks tend to lay a couple of hours after daybreak. As the weather improves, make sure it is not too warm in the house and don't keep her in after about 9 am. Collect the eggs each day as soon as possible after laying, to prevent them from getting dirty or a magpie or crow collecting them for you!

For a goose, you can provide a nest area, which should be in place well before the time you expect the bird to start laying. It should be about 2 ft (60 cm) square and filled with nesting material such as straw. If the goose house is big enough, try positioning a couple of bales of straw in a corner with a space between them for her to enter and be private. An old dog or cat house, large feeding container or simply plenty of bedding in the corner of the house may suffice. Don't skimp on the nesting material and make sure it is kept dry. You can collect the eggs if you don't want the bird to breed; if you do, let them accumulate until she is ready to sit.

Collecting and storing eggs

Once your birds are laying, you should collect the eggs daily (see page 42) and store them in a clean, cool place. You may like to wash them too. It's a good idea to record the number laid each day on a calendar (see page 42). Get friends to bring you their empty eggboxes and store your eggs in them, marking each box with the laying date.

There is still a fear of salmonella in relation to ducks eggs that dates all the way back to World War II. This is largely unfair – as with any egg, the advice is that pregnant woman, children, elderly people and those who are sick should only eat eggs if they are cooked thoroughly. With any egg-producing bird, hygiene in the all areas (house, run, and egg store) is paramount.

Selling your surplus

If you have cared for your birds well, you may have a surplus of eggs that you would like to sell. Before you do, check out the latest government regulations to make sure you can comply. Always take care not to sell any cracked, dirty, or damaged eggs, and make sure you know the date on which they were laid.

You can try selling your eggs to friends and work colleagues or at a farmers' market. Display them attractively, perhaps in a basket against clean straw with a picture of the ducks. You will soon have customers returning regularly for more!

Above Display your beautiful eggs, ready to be sold at markets or to friends and family.

Pests and Diseases

Ducks and geese are naturally healthy birds and should remain so if kept in suitable conditions and fed appropriately. Generally prevention is far better than cure, although there are some ailments from which they are more likely to suffer at some time in their lives.

Health checks

Set aside time each day to check over your birds carefully. You don't have to handle them – some simple observational checks will help you to spot any potential problems. You can then examine any suspect bird individually and take action.

Observing your birds

The most important thing you can do is know what is normal for your birds (see pages 42–45). Noticing unusual behavior at an early stage will give you an indication that a problem may be brewing, so do not ignore it.

When you let the birds out of their house, they should be eager and excited, greeting the day as if it were a totally new experience. Any bird that remains in the house should be examined; during the breeding season she could be going broody rather than feeling unwell, but you need to make sure. Watch out for a bird sitting for long periods or moving slowly and stopping often. Watch, too, for stragglers – they could be feeling unwell and unable to keep up with the flock.

The birds should be keen to eat the food you give them. If one hangs back, examine it more closely. At the very least, it could be the victim of bullying and therefore not be getting enough to eat; at worst, it could be in discomfort.

Ducks in particular love water, so if a bird is reluctant to enter the pond or simply ignores it, this is a possible sign of distress.

Further examination

If you are concerned about any bird, your next job is to catch it and examine it with your hands. Unfortunately, birds generally do not show major symptoms until an illness is well in progress. It is therefore likely when you handle the bird that you will find it has dropped weight and feels thin with a sharp, protruding breastbone. The bird will feel light when you lift it up.

Isolation

Your next task is to isolate the bird from the flock to prevent any possible spread of disease. This will also eliminate the danger of other birds trampling the sick one or making it move when it is suffering.

It's a good idea to have an isolation area already prepared for just such an eventuality, so that you can act swiftly. If you haven't, you will need to make a dry, clean pen as quickly as possible using boards, hurdles or straw bales. You may have to pen a goose or gander with their mate, or at least so that they can see them, as they can become very distressed when separated. Place clean water in the pen and provide a nutritious ration, such as a good compound feed, and some grit. If the bird refuses to eat, you may have to try some grain or green food to encourage it.

Observation and action

If the bird is not obviously suffering, then observe it at regular intervals and if it does not get better within 24 hours contact your vet. If other birds show the same symptoms, do the same. If the bird recovers, you still need to discover the cause of the illness and eliminate it. It's not always possible to get to the root of the problem, but it is worth making every effort to do so.

Finally, record the incident on your calendar, so that if anything similar happens again you can compare the two. Good observation will stop disease from progressing through the flock or an injury from becoming untreatable as it worsens. It is never an option to just hope that it might improve.

Eyes should be bright. Dull eyes indicate the bird is feeling unwell.

Discharge may mean you are not providing enough water for the bird to wash its head, or may be an early symptom of another problem.

Plumage should be shiny and well oiled through preening. If dull, the bird is not feeling well enough to care for itself or does not have access to sufficient splashing water for it to be able to preen.

Vent should be clean – waste matter clinging to the feathers clearly indicates something is wrong.

Check that the bird is not lame or limping. Check that the bird is walking normally, not in an uncoordinated or confused manner.

Pests and Diseases

Left The correct way to hold a duck for examination.

Keeping your birds healthy

Disease prevention is about good management. Follow the guidelines below to give your flock the best chance of living long, healthy lives.

- Don't overstock. It's far better to keep fewer birds than an area will support than too many. The tighter the stocking ratio, the more intensive and accurate the management must be.
- Obtain strong, healthy stock and don't mix birds from different sources. Disease can be brought in from shows and sales, and birds that are not carefully introduced may be injured by the existing flock.
- If you buy additional birds, keep them separate from the flock for at least two weeks. When you introduce them, follow a sympathetic procedure (see pages 84–85).
- Feed a well-balanced ration that is not moldy or out of date.

- Provide plenty of clean water and change the water in small ponds regularly.
- Watch out for rats: they can carry disease and must be controlled (see pages 38–39).
- Make sure grass areas are clean and rotated regularly.
- Make sure your birds cannot gain access to poisonous substances such as garden chemicals like slug pellets. This is especially important if your ducks are helping to clear your garden of pests.
- Keep grassland free of twine and plastic bags, and fishing line if your birds are on a river.
- If the birds graze with other animals, ensure that licks, minerals, and wormers used for them are not harmful to the flock.
- Provide shade in summer and shelter in winter.
- Feed and water young birds before you see to the more mature stock as they are more susceptible to disease.

- Put young birds on pasture that has not been used recently by older birds.
- Keep the bird house clean and dry.
- You may need to adopt a regular deworming program.
- Keep feeders, drinkers, and any other equipment clean.
- Provide insoluble grit so that the gizzard can function properly – essential if the birds do not have a reasonable-sized range.
- Check for external parasites regularly.
- Handle your birds calmly and get to know them.
- Keep boisterous dogs and children away from the flock.
- Get to know a veterinarian who specializes in poultry and keep their telephone number to hand.
- Always present a bird to the veterinarian with a full history including age, sex, management and feed details, and breeding record. Be accurate about when the disease first appeared and the symptoms.

Death and euthanasia

It is a sad fact of keeping any livestock that you will also have deadstock. Any unexpected deaths should be removed quickly from the flock and every effort made to pinpoint the cause.

You will need access to someone who can dispatch birds quickly. Having a bird suffer and die slowly is not acceptable. Consult your veterinarian for information on euthanasia.

If one of your birds dies it is, of course, distressing. Many small-scale duck and goose keepers allow their birds to live out their natural lifespan, so deaths are inevitable. Try to learn from any early deaths and feel pleased that you have been able to give older birds a rich and enjoyable life. Grieve for them, but don't feel guilty.

Right A healthy bird has bright eyes and an alert expression.

Parasites

All livestock attract parasites, but action can and should be taken to prevent internal infestations and to protect against external pests. Know your enemy by taking time to learn about the parasites that affect ducks and geese and how to spot them.

Internal parasites
The life cycle of a parasite is completed within a bird and uses that bird's body for sustenance and life.

Gape worms
So-called because the afflicted bird quite literally gasps for breath, these parasites are more commonly seen in chickens but can also affect ducks and geese. The bird may appear quite normal in every other way but the condition should not be ignored. The gape worm

(*Cyathostoma bronchialis*) is transmitted from the grass, so it is likely that other birds in the flock will also be affected. Treat with a proprietary wormer following your vet's advice.

Gizzard worms
These very unpleasant parasites burrow into the gizzard, causing considerable damage and distress. Severe weight loss and lethargy may occur, and there may be red flecks in the droppings. If the worm is

Above Parasites can be the cause when a duck is dull and listless.

Above Excessive scratching is a symptom of external parasites.

present in the area in great numbers it may affect ducks, but it is the major worm to watch out for in geese. This is because it is transmitted from the birds' droppings via the grassland. Geese graze more than ducks, so are more susceptible. The young and old are always more vulnerable and you can easily lose goslings (or ducklings) to this preventable worm. Treat with a proprietary wormer following your vet's advice.

Round worms

These are transmitted via the soil or an infected insect. A large burden will damage the bird's digestive system, causing weight loss, listlessness, and even upsetting the immune system, making it vulnerable to disease. Treat with a proprietary wormer following your vet's advice. A change in management should also be considered.

External parasites

Parasites that live in the bird's feathers and on the skin cause considerable irritation and can also suck blood which will debilitate the bird. Check regularly for them.

Red mite

This is a common and increasing problem for chicken keepers. Part of the reason is that in the past people would buy laying hens, keep them for a year, and then kill them, clean the house thoroughly, and restock. These days, many people keep their hens for much longer, sometimes way beyond their useful life. This gives the red mite a real chance to get established in hen houses, where it lies dormant in the wood and crevices waiting for a nice, warm bird to come in so that it can feed on its blood.

Ducks and geese are a lot less prone to these greedy little bloodsuckers, but you should still wash out their house at least annually and use a spray that kills this mite. It's a good idea to remove the birds for a night or so at this time, although there are sprays available that are harmless to birds. Follow the instructions carefully and always ensure that anything you use is safe for waterfowl. If you have a major infestation, you will have to obtain a powder to put directly on the birds.

Northern mite
This is more of a problem as it does seem to affect waterfowl, although mainly around the head area. It is also incredibly persistent. If goslings or ducklings have

Above Watch your birds carefully for signs of distress or irritation.

been raised by a broody hen, it is vital to ensure that she is absolutely clear of all mites, especially these. Treat as for red mite, but you may need to repeat the treatment.

Leeches and ticks
Remove these when you see them, using tweezers and taking care to remove the mouth parts. Think about which area of your land is harboring these pests and deal with the problem, following professional advice.

Maggots (fly strike)
These tend to affect sick, old, or injured birds and occur when a fly lays eggs into a wound or around the vent when there is a discharge. Remove the maggots with tweezers and apply antiseptic, but also look for the cause of the infestation such as insufficient water, a digestive problem, or an untreated wound. Maggots may also enter more deeply into the body than you can see, for example via the vent, and may now be internal. If this is the case, you should euthanize the bird quickly as it will suffer. Be particularly vigilant for this problem during hot, moist spells of weather.

Worms and wormers

Many of the internal parasite problems that occur in ducks and geese can be prevented by adopting a regular worming program.

Wormers are usually administered in drinking water. Herbal wormers are now available in pellet form. Whichever you choose, you need to follow the instructions carefully as an insufficient dose will not eradicate the worm burden.

As well as using wormers, preventing worms is a matter of management. Don't overstock, mix different ages if possible, and, most importantly, keep grassland clean by rotation.

Common ailments

Ducks and geese are hardy creatures, but recognizing any problems that do occur at an early stage often makes treatment easier and the outcome more successful. The following is a guide to some of the most common complaints you may encounter.

Lameness
Lameness in waterfowl, however slight, means that you should carefully examine the bird.

Bumblefoot
This is by far the most common condition causing lameness in waterfowl. It is a large swelling caused by bacteria and probably triggered by a small injury such as a bruise or stepping on something sharp. This is why it is important to have smooth surfaces around your bird house and ponds and soft ground. It is quite hard to cure, although you can try bathing the foot and checking for an entrance to the original wound, or giving the bird a course of antibiotics. The bird will need confinement on a clean, soft surface and if the wound can be drained it will need bathing regularly. It may be necessary to seek veterinary advice. Depending on the severity, some birds can live with bumblefoot; others will have to be euthanized if it is causing them severe discomfort.

Calluses and abrasions
The cause here is walking on sharp surfaces. Apply antibiotic cream and keep the bird on a soft bed until the area has healed. Prompt treatment to a minor wound will avoid bumblefoot. You will also need to deal with the cause.

Broken leg
Legs can be strained to the point of breaking due to difficulty getting in or out of the water (so change the ramp) or through fighting. Another cause is a heavy male repeatedly mating with a small female – drakes are particularly guilty of this, and any offender should be removed so he can do no further harm. Seek veterinary advice immediately, although with a very bad break it is advisable to euthanize the bird as quickly as possible. Following treatment, the bird should be rested in an isolation pen until it is able to walk freely again.

Breathing problems
Fungal spores cause aspergillosis, which shows as heavy, labored breathing. It thrives in damp litter, moldy bedding, and moldy bread or food. It is therefore easily preventable. Use only clean, sweet-smelling straw – if it makes you cough, discard it.

Above Always confine a lame bird and try to establish the cause.

Wood shavings are a good alternative for bedding.
Other diseases in which labored breathing is a symptom include the notifiable Newcastle disease and avian flu (see pages 70–71). These are not common, so examine other causes and possibilities first.

Digestive problems

Any really foul-smelling, excessively watery droppings, and particularly those with blood in them, must be treated with suspicion.

Coccidiosis

These are parasites that live in the lining of the bird's intestine. It means that the intestine is unable to function properly and cannot absorb the nutrients from food, so the bird becomes thin. Chickens tend to suffer more than waterfowl but they may still be affected, especially the young. A vet can discover how bad the infestation is by taking a sample of the infected droppings, and it can then be treated with an anticoccidial. Although not always caused by overcrowded, dirty conditions, this is a factor in many cases so change your management.

Enteritis

This covers all manner of violent digestive disorders, caused by either bacteria or a virus. Symptoms are

Above Sudden death should always be investigated and the remaining birds carefully observed.

lethargy and diarrhea. In both types, prevention is down to good hygiene, and denying wild birds (which may be carriers) access to feed and water – which will, of course, be near impossible with a pond, stream, or river. Consult your vet immediately, as treatment must be prompt.

Impaction (crop binding)

This is a good reason for ensuring your goose pastures are free from garden string or plastic, as the foreign body may lodge in the upper part of the digestive system. It can also be caused by gizzard worms, or result when there is insufficient grit for the gizzard to function as it should. The upper part of the breast area will be swollen and feel hard to the touch. The bird will be off its food and look miserable. Gentle massage might remove the impaction, but in severe cases your vet will need to operate.

Botulism

Particularly prevalent in warm weather, the source of the bacteria that cause botulism is usually stagnant ponds, bogs, or decaying waste. It causes toxicity and the sick bird will lose control of its neck muscles so that the head lies on the ground – that is why it's also called limberneck. Death can occur within hours. You might be able to save a mild case by isolating the bird and giving plenty of fresh water. Then give supportive treatment including tempting feed and rest. A course of antibiotics may help. It goes without saying that you should find and remove the source of the outbreak.

Plumage problems

Feathers are extremely important to the bird for warmth, protection, and in some cases, flight.

Molting

This is natural at certain times of year, depending on the breed, climate, and so on. Feathers don't last forever and are replaced – in its natural environment, the bird needs good, strong feathers for flight and warmth. It also needs to attract a mate, and males will molt into their courtship plumage and back again after breeding. At this time they can look very shabby indeed and quite sorry for themselves. Because losing feathers interferes with flight, even if the bird does not fly naturally it will probably appear more timid at this time. Provide supportive feeding with a balanced ration throughout molting.

Feather pecking

In young birds, this is caused by boredom or bullying. They need something to occupy them, such as food to peck at and plenty of space. In older birds, the causes are bullying (remove the bully), parasites, or mating. The back of a duck's neck usually loses some feathers during mating, but if the skin is broken then either she or the drake should be removed. A further cause in all ages can be a deficiency in the diet.

Wing deformities

Slipped wing (angel wing) occurs in goslings and ducklings that are a few weeks old and appears in fast-growing birds that may be receiving too much protein. If you see a wing begin to hang down, immediately reduce the level of protein in the diet and tape the wing into place. Act quickly or you will not be able to correct the condition.

Eye problems

If a bird's eyes are red, sticky, or weepy, be absolutely sure that it has access to clean water where it can wash its head and neck. Next check for parasites. Finally, if both of these causes can be eliminated you may need to treat with antibiotic cream. Watch the rest of the flock to ensure the problem does not spread.

Problems associated with egg production

Egg laying is a complicated process for the body but waterfowl do seem not to suffer as much as chickens.

Ask the experts

Although it is important to isolate a sick bird and offer supportive treatments, you should not prolong the life of a bird when there is no suitable treatment. It is not an option to do nothing, with the bird becoming increasingly unwell. Veterinary advice should be sought sooner rather than later – for new duck or goose keepers, money spent on veterinary advice is an investment for the future as it will increase your knowledge. Go straight to a real expert, get the answer and then follow the treatment or euthanize the bird promptly. The bird's welfare should always be your priority.

Egg binding

This is a nasty condition in which the bird cannot pass an egg. If the egg is almost ready to be laid and near the vent you can help by applying warm olive oil or vaseline around the vent and gently helping to ease out the egg – conditions need to be warm to relax the muscles. If this cannot be completed easily, you need to seek veterinary advice. This may include breaking the egg in order to remove it, which is best done by the vet. Antibiotics will be needed afterwards.

Prolapse

In female birds, you will see part of the oviduct protruding from the vent; in drakes, the penis cannot retract. Both sexes should be removed from the flock. You may be able to replace a mild prolapse of the oviduct gently or it might even retract on its own, as might the penis. However, more usually there is nothing you can do, and if there is no improvement after a few days of supportive care the bird should be euthanized.

Pests and Diseases

Avian flu

This disease has recently hit the headlines, although it has actually been around for at least 100 years and was first recognized in the US in 1924. More recently, an outbreak in the Netherlands brought avian flu back to prominence.

Precautions

There are two types of avian influenza: low pathogenic (LPAI) and highly pathogenic (HPAI). It is the H5N1 strain of the latter that is a major cause for concern as there have been cases of human infection and even death. A vaccine is available, but policy on its use varies from country to country. If there is a cull policy, you will not be able to vaccinate your birds.

The way this book suggests keeping ducks and geese will keep the risk of infection from birds to human very low indeed. The disease can only spread if birds and people are in very close contact over periods of time. If there is an outbreak of avian flu in your area, you should not be alarmed for your own or your family's safety. Follow the instructions given by your state veterinary department for your birds.

Unfortunately, these are likely to include bringing your ducks and geese indoors away from wild birds. This is particularly difficult where waterfowl are concerned, as you will have to provide access to water for welfare which will cause a great deal of mess. You should identify suitable buildings where you can manage this without causing too much distress to your birds, or have plans for enclosing a reasonable-sized run with bird-dropping-proof mesh. This is another good reason not to overstock, in case you have to house all your birds in a hurry.

Left In an outbreak of avian flu even commercial free-range flocks may have to be brought inside to stop it from spreading.

Recognizing avian flu

Like Newcastle disease (see box, right), avian flu is a notifiable disease and you must therefore contact your state agricultural department immediately if you suspect an outbreak.

You should be suspicious if there are a large number of sudden deaths among your birds. HPAI shows itself suddenly with swelling of the head, dullness, lack of appetite, severe breathing problems, diarrhea, and a marked drop in egg production. These symptoms must be taken very seriously.

What is bio-security?

The importance of good bio-security is mentioned repeatedly in the prevention of avian flu. This involves practicing much of what has already been described in this book: cleanliness, careful observation, and not overstocking. As this disease is spread through the movement of poultry, people, and vehicles, and with wild birds – especially migratory – also implicated, the following measures should be observed:

- Keep feed away from wild birds.
- Keep water fresh, clear of droppings and, as far as possible, prevent access by wild birds and vermin such as rats.
- Isolate all new stock from your existing flock for at least three weeks.
- Know where any new stock has originated.
- Don't bring infection on to your premises, especially if there is an outbreak in your area. If you have been to a show or sale, change your clothes and boots, and wash before you handle your waterfowl.
- Keep transport crates and boxes clean, and if you use cardboard boxes dispose of them after use.

Unfortunately, it seems that avian flu is something we and our birds will have to live with for the foreseeable future, so the best we can do is to follow the measures suggested here and be ready to take any action required in the event of an outbreak.

Newcastle disease

This is a notifiable disease in many countries. The clinical signs in affected birds can be very variable. The disease can be present in a very acute form with sudden onset and high mortality, or as a mild disease shown as some breathing difficulties or maybe a drop in egg numbers. General clinical signs include depression, lack of appetite, respiratory distress with beak gaping, coughing, sneezing, gurgling and rattling, yellowish green diarrhea, and nervous signs. In laying flocks, a sudden drop in egg production with a high proportion laid with abnormal (soft) shells is often an early sign. Young birds are particularly susceptible and mortality can be heavy, with survivors often exhibiting permanent nervous problems.

Above If a country has a cull policy then vaccinatation of your flock is not an option.

Pests and Diseases

Hatching and Rearing

One of the cutest sights imaginable is a baby duckling or gosling. But how practical is it to breed your own waterfowl? There are several different ways to hatch eggs and rear young birds, so it's a matter of choosing the one that is right for your situation.

Breeding from your own birds

It is a natural part of the waterfowl's world to court and breed. Unlike hybrid hens, a duck or goose has the instinct to want to breed and rear young, albeit with varying degrees of success. Not every breed, or individual bird, is a successful mother.

Preparing to breed

The breeding season begins from late winter onwards, when the males are in full plumage. The males become more possessive and fights can break out if you have too many. You should select which are going to be allowed to breed, and remove the rest. You should not just allow different breeds to mate with no real idea of which birds laid or fertilized the eggs.

Water

In the very heavy breeds of duck, water is essential for successful mating. Although other breeds may be more fertile if they have access to water, they can manage adequately enough on land. Geese – especially the heavier breeds – prefer to mate in water, although they too may manage to mate successfully on land.

Left Always choose the best specimens you can for breeding.

Mating

Ducks and geese are very different in their approach to pairing and mating. By understanding their natural behaviors, you can help to ensure mating is both safe and successful.

Ducks

Drakes have considerable libido and will mate with anything and everything they can, although Call ducks tend to form more obvious family groups.

Unlike a cockerel, a drake does have a penis so you need to be especially careful that he does not overmate with a female: a drake will mate repeatedly, pulling out feathers from the duck's head and neck as well as possibly causing internal damage. It is therefore vital that you have the right ratio of drakes to ducks. If you want to keep rather than cull surplus drakes, you will need to remove most of them to a bachelor pen where they will settle down together, away from the females. Ideally you need one drake to six or more ducks for the lighter breeds; the heavier breeds are a little slower and you may get away with an extra drake.

Watch the female birds closely for signs of distress. Sometimes one duck will be mated repeatedly, causing her great distress and internal injuries. Remove either her or the drake, and replace him a few days later with a less active male. You must not leave a female to be injured in this way.

Geese

Quite different to ducks, geese form the strongest bond between male and female in domestic fowl. They grieve if a mate dies and often won't accept another for quite some time.

The number of females to males varies with the breed. Four geese to a gander is about the maximum, but some breeds prefer a one-to-one ratio. Although a goose can rear young in her first year, her eggs and goslings may be smaller so it might be better to wait until her second year.

Hatching and Rearing

Breeding checklist

✔ Always breed the very best birds you can by selecting the best parents.

✔ Make a plan for the offspring. If they are to be sold, you must produce really good examples of the breed.

✔ Don't allow different breeds to interbreed. Before mating takes place, separate them into designated breeding areas.

✔ Make sure you have the right number of males for your breed – surplus males cause fights, may injure females and can interfere with breeding pairs.

✔ Heavy breeds may need water for successful mating, something you should consider when you choose a breed.

✔ Feed the birds a balanced breeder's ration. Put geese on fresh grass and provide green food for ducks.

✔ Don't breed from very young or very old birds. It will be unsuccessful and cause distress.

✔ Keep records of when mating commences, when eggs are laid, and any action you have had to take such as removing drakes.

✔ Don't let the birds themselves railroad you into breeding before you are ready to cope with the resulting young. It is better to remove and use eggs than have ducklings or goslings without sufficient facilities for them.

✔ Don't attempt to breed until you are happy caring for and handling your adult birds. And don't breed if you are short of time to care for the youngsters or, most importantly, if you are short of space. It's up to you to control who breeds with whom, when and how often.

Incubation

Should you do what comes naturally with a broody duck or goose, or is it a better idea to use an incubator? This section explains how to make your choice and then have the best chance of producing live, healthy duckling or goslings.

This involves the female bird brooding her own eggs and raising the young. In an ideal world, this is the best scenario. All you have to do is provide optimum conditions and then leave the bird to it. In practice, not all birds are natural mothers.

Above A duck is not too fussy about where she lays her eggs but cleanliness is important.

Domestic ducks are not the best sitters – they are not as inclined to stay on the eggs as geese or hens. High egg-laying breeds of duck such as Khaki Campbells or Runners are not particularly broody, but there is always the exception that proves the rule. Ducks of all breeds tend to become more flighty when they are broody – hens usually sit tight despite whatever is going on around them.

Ducks

You'll know when your duck is broody. She will lay a clutch of eggs – that is, spend consecutive days laying into the same nest but not sitting – until she feels she has enough. It could be as much as ten or as few as two. She will then sit on them. They will not start to develop until she sits tight, remaining on her eggs day and night and getting up only briefly to find a minimum of food and water. You will see feathers around the nest area and the bird will hiss and become very protective.

If you want a duck to stay on her eggs, you need to ensure her safety. If she is not in the house or a secure run, you will literally need to build one around her, at least until the eggs have hatched and you can move her and the ducklings.

Don't forget that magpies, crows, and rats will take unprotected eggs and even very small ducklings. You can try moving the duck to somewhere secure but generally only a small percentage adapt – the others just give up and go back to where they wanted to be. Water and food will need to be close at hand, including water for washing. Keep drakes away.

When sitting, the duck will keep the eggs at a constant temperature, turn them and keep them at the right humidity – if and when you use an incubator, you will really appreciate her efforts! It's at this time that you really will be rewarded if you have managed to tame your ducks, as it's far easier to deal with a duck that knows and trusts you than a semi-wild and nervous one that is naturally quite excited by the experience.

The disadvantage of natural brooding is that you have to trust the duck. That's fine if she really does know more than you do, but many problems can arise. These include her getting off the eggs early, or hatching a couple of ducklings and then moving,

Above Some geese breeds such as the Toulouse are not naturally very broody.

leaving the others half-hatched. There are often genuine reasons why birds get off eggs, ranging from parasites to the fact that they realize the eggs are non-viable, but equally often there seems to be no reason at all. Any bird can be allowed one failure, but a persistent offender who frequently loses interest should not be allowed to keep sitting. Take the eggs away and quickly put them in an incubator or under a hen. An egg that has been sat on (brooded) for a period and then left to go very cold will not continue to develop.

Geese

Although more reliable than ducks, geese have their share of problems as well. Some breeds, such as the Toulouse, are not keen to go broody. Being heavy, they – and the Embdens and Africans – also tend to trample eggs or, worse still, young goslings. Your job is to provide the right conditions for the goose to feel comfortable to go broody, in the form of an encouraging-looking nest in a secluded part of the house. She may well then choose somewhere completely unsuitable (to your eyes) under a hedge or shrub, and you will have to decide if you can make the area secure enough for her to continue in her quest. The area needs to be dry so you may need to put a tent over it, some bedding inside, and food and water nearby so that she doesn't have to get up and leave her eggs. The nest and goose must be safe from predators.

Unlike with a duck, there is no need to remove a goose's mate, but don't allow other ganders into the area. It is important to worm the goose when she shows signs of being broody so that she doesn't pass on worms to the youngsters and also gets maximum nutrition from her food. A broody bird of any kind will lose weight while she is sitting, which is why providing nutritious food close by is so important.

Using a broody hen

A hen can raise ducklings and goslings for you. The Silkie is the traditional choice for a broody because they love being mothers. Crossbred Silkies are probably the ideal, but if you have hens yourself you will soon identify individuals that spend the spring and summer in a perpetual state of broodiness. You can encourage them by placing pot eggs in a suitable nest, but your best bet is to take a hen that has gone broody already and is sitting tight. Gently remove her eggs in the evening, as early in the broody period as possible, and replace with the eggs you want her to hatch.

Although the incubation periods for duck, goose, and hen eggs are different (see box, below), fortunately hens tend to sit until the egg hatches rather than having a cut-off point at 21 days. The thing that will put a hen off most is parasites, and hens are much more prone to these when brooding than are ducks or geese. Often when a hen leaves her eggs you can see that they are covered with little specks of red, clearly indicating the presence of red mite (see pages 65–66). You cannot expect her to sit and quite literally be eaten alive by these irritating and dangerous bloodsuckers.

Do not put any more eggs under the hen than she can cover, as they will get cold and die. The exact number will naturally vary according to the size of eggs and of the hen.

Hatching times

Bantams 19–21 days

Chickens 21 days

Ducks 28 days

Muscovies 35–37 days

Geese 28–35 (depending on breed)

Checking the eggs

Providing the broody bird is reasonably tame, you should be able to examine the eggs quietly. A gander may be less obliging when he sees you near his and his mate's eggs. Otherwise, you will have to wait until the bird leaves the nest to eat – something broodies often do very early in the morning. You can candle the eggs to see how they are developing (see page 82). Always remove any obviously rotten eggs.

If you feel that to look at the eggs would distress the duck or goose, then leave them alone. However, if there are no signs of ducklings or goslings a few days after the expected date, you will have to examine the eggs to make absolutely sure nothing is happening and then remove them. Otherwise, the bird will continue to sit at detriment to her health and with no resulting youngsters.

It is much easier to check the eggs with a broody hen, as she is far less easily disturbed and will probably be more indignant than scared at your intervention. Don't let her continue if the eggs are not going to hatch – she will already have exceeded her natural 21 days and will have lost a considerable amount of weight.

Artificial incubation

To have more control over the eggs and when they are hatched, and to have more chance of getting young from a bird that may not go broody, an artificial incubator is the better choice. However, although modern incubators are technically superb, when natural incubation goes smoothly it will produce an almost 100 percent hatch of healthy young, so for many people the broody is still the preferred choice.

With an incubator, results will only be as good as the stability of the outside air conditions, your ability to follow the manufacturer's instructions to the letter, the quality of the eggs that you put into it, and the cleanliness of the incubator. Even if you adhere strictly

Left A broody hen sits on her
eggs for 21 days but is happy
to sit for 28 days to hatch
ducklings.

79

Hatching and Rearing

to these requirements, you may still have some
failures, which is why maintaining detailed records
for incubation will help you to gain knowledge for the
future. Remember, too, that manufacturers are keen
for their machines to be successful, so talk through
any failures with them and then adjust the machine
as necessary for the next hatch.

Types of incubator
There are many different incubators available, from
small "home" sizes to vast industrial machines that are
expected to hatch effectively many times for their
commercial clients. As with any machine, you get what
you pay for, but you don't need to go to the largest
capacity or top of the range for your first incubator. As

incubators run better full, spare capacity is not a good
idea. You will need to decide between still air and
forced air (fan assisted), and manual, semi-automatic,
and fully automatic models.

Still air Put simply, this is an insulated box with a
heating element and is very carefully designed to
avoid hot and cold spots. A thermostat maintains
the temperature.

Forced air or fan assisted Again, this is an insulated
box with a thermostat, but this time a fan causes the
air to circulate evenly and allows you to have several
layers of eggs if necessary. This machine is more
expensive than a still-air incubator.

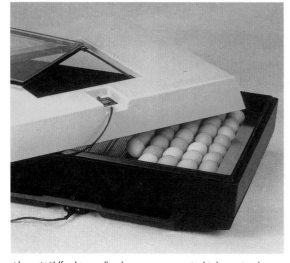

Above Wildfowl, as well as hen, eggs can go in this larger incubator.

Above A small incubator, perfect for beginners to use.

Manual A broody turns her eggs every day to prevent the embryo sticking to the shell and allow it to access nutrients evenly. The eggs in an incubator have to be turned in opposite directions at least three times a day and this must be maintained from 24 hours after setting (putting the eggs in the incubator) until two days before hatching. Given that the developmental period is at least 28 days, this is an absolute commitment for 25 days.

Semi-automatic With this design the eggs still need to be turned, but instead of doing this individually by hand a handle allows you to turn a whole tray of eggs from the outside. You still have to commit to doing this at least three times a day.

Fully automatic The incubator turns the eggs, several times a day. You don't have to remember to do this and the eggs are turned more frequently, without having to open the incubator at all. These last two types are more expensive than a manual machine, but not necessarily prohibitively.

In addition, you will need to decide between buying an incubator with a built-in hatcher or using both an incubator and a hatcher. For beginners, it is better to start with a machine that combines the two.

Using the incubator

Successful hatching begins with selecting the right egg and storing it properly until you put it in the incubator. Eggs must be collected daily and immediately stored at 53.6–60.8°F (12–16°C). If you store them in a warm place the embryo will try to develop and then die, so the egg will be useless when transferred to the incubator. Clean egg trays are suitable for storing the eggs, place them in point down. Eggs lose moisture even before they are placed in the incubator, so make sure the atmosphere is not too dry. Do not store eggs for longer than ten days and don't put eggs that have recently been laid into the incubator – allow them to settle for at least 24 hours first. If you have transported the eggs – perhaps bought them from a sale or even through the mail – allow them to settle for a day. When selecting eggs, discard any that are:

- Cracked – these will not hatch and could introduce bacteria to healthy eggs.
- Thin shelled or with shells that are not smooth.
- Double yolkers – these show as oversized eggs for the breed.
- Oddly shaped, such as being long and thin or too round.
- Small for the breed, as often laid by young birds.

The incubator should have already been disinfected and run for at least a day so that the temperature is even. Place the eggs in a warm but not hot room for a few hours so they are not cold going into the incubator. Don't heat them up: they need be only a few degrees above cold, and cold is better than too hot. When you are ready, put the eggs into the incubator, close the lid and check for draughts.

Finally, check the thermometer as filling the machine can alter the temperature and you may have to make an adjustment.

Make a note of the day you put the eggs in and the time. It can be useful to record the weather daily, as the temperature of the room and the humidity surrounding the incubator does make a difference to the hatch.

Candling

This involves shining a bright light through the eggshell so that it shows what is happening inside. A bright torch will do the job, but purpose-designed candlers are available from incubator manufacturers

Left Organic eggs being placed into the incubator.

Incubator checklist

✔ If you buy secondhand, be sure to clean the machine with a suitable incubator disinfectant before use. It's a good idea to wipe down a new one as well, and always clean between hatches or when putting an incubator away until the following year. The warm, moist environment is ideal for hatching not only eggs but also bacteria.

✔ Site the incubator carefully. It must not be disturbed, nor subject to extremes of temperature or humidity, as this will affect the machine and therefore the hatch. It must be placed on a level surface. Keep the incubator away from other people who might interfere with the controls or keep opening it to look.

✔ Follow the manufacturer's instructions on adding water for humidity. Eggs must lose water in order to form a viable air sac and therefore eventually hatch, but they also need some humidity. Getting the balance right will depend on outside conditions as well. You may not need to add any water earlier in the year, depending on the weather.

✔ Check the recommended temperature in the machine's manual, but as a guide it should be around 99.5°F (37.5°C) for duck and goose eggs.

embryo continues to form, the air sac at the broad end of the egg will grow in size, so that by the last few days it will take up about one-third of the egg. A small air sac means that there is too much moisture in the air (so the egg is not losing enough), while an over-large air sac means that there is too little. Both conditions will lead to the embryo dying in the shell.

Although it is tempting to keep candling the eggs, having looked initially, do not check them more than weekly, so as not to disturb the incubator temperature. Don't worry if you are not sure whether the air sac is the correct size – this is something you will learn to spot as you gain more experience. To begin with, just look for a gradually increasing air sac at the thick end of the egg, which develops more rapidly towards the hatch date.

Hatching

Using your records and consulting the manufacturer's recommendations, the incubator with a built-in hatcher must now become the hatcher. Just before the eggs begin to hatch, stop turning and replace the rollers with a hatching tray or transfer eggs to a hatcher. Check the suggested temperature for hatching, which can be a little lower than at the incubation stage.

Before hatching comes the pipping stage, when the hatchling begins to break through the shell. Do not attempt to help it and do not open the incubator. It can take a day or so for a duckling to emerge and longer for a gosling. As you become more experienced there may be times when intervention is possible, but if you help a duckling or gosling and blood begins to run, stop immediately. Most hatchlings that are going to live are able to get out of the shell on their own. If they can't, they may not be fit enough to survive the next stage.

Leave the youngsters in the hatcher for a rest of 24 hours or so following hatching, then remove them to the rearing pen. They are wet when they emerge,

and these are easy to use and relatively inexpensive. If you are planning to do a lot of incubation, it is well worth investing in one.

Once the eggs are in the incubator, candling at five to seven days will tell you if they are developing or are clear (that is, no embryo is forming). At five to seven days you should see red veins developing. As the so they need to dry. Any eggs not hatched can be left for a few more days, but a quick candling will tell you what is happening.

Dead in shell

This is possibly the most distressing and certainly a very common problem, and all you can do is learn from it. The most usual reasons for dead in shell – which is where the fully formed duckling or gosling dies before it can emerge – is too much or too little humidity; the embryo developing either in the wrong position so that it cannot move to "pip"; or with a deformity; overheating of the incubator or hatcher; or weak embryos from small eggs. This is where your records will help you to establish the cause, as will an examination of the egg contents. Even people who have been incubating for many years have disastrous hatches, and the best thing to do is to learn from them.

Above After successfully hatching your eggs you can move on to rearing your ducklings or goslings.

Rearing ducklings and goslings

The egg has successfully developed into a duckling or gosling, and now the youngster has to be provided with optimum conditions, not only to maintain life but to enable it to grow up healthy and strong.

A caring mother?

If the duck or goose hatched the eggs herself, you now need to make sure she is going to care for them. First-time mothers, in particular, may seem confused by their hatchlings and veer from overprotective, often treading on them in the course of their efforts, to casual, where life simply carries on as before. When nature works, though, it is fantastic and the duck or goose will bring up her young proudly. Your contribution will be to give them a safe environment, away from the rest of the flock (except the goose's mate) and predators including hawks, and to provide feed and water.

Feeding

For the first few weeks, it is essential to spend time observing that everything is going well. Confine the

Above Muscovy duck caring for her ducklings.

birds to a house or shed of suitable size, making sure they are not cramped, until the goslings or ducklings are big enough to walk well, feed and drink.

Begin with starter crumbs (see page 51). For geese, you will have to ensure that the adults don't eat them all first, as the goslings need the nutrition. An arrangement whereby the goslings can get in to feed but the geese can't (a creep feeder for lambs uses the same principle) works well. For ducks, if you provide crumbs and wheat, the duck will soon tire of the crumb and stick to eating the wheat, leaving the ducklings the crumbs – but you still need to make sure they are getting sufficient feed.

Water

For the first few days, you will need to provide water in a way that ensures the ducklings or goslings cannot drown – a shallow container with a brick in it ensures the container cannot move or tip. It also provides refuge if a duckling or gosling falls in: a very young bird could easily become exhausted trying to get out and then drown or die of cold. After a few days provide more water, but still using a brick.

If you used a hen for hatching you need to be aware that she will not be able to provide the preen oil necessary for the waterfowl to be waterproof. Until their own preen glands work, if they try to swim they will become waterlogged and drown. Keep broody-reared or incubated waterfowl away from swimming or total immersion in water until they are at least a month old.

Clean and safe

Try to keep the brooding area clean, but don't upset the birds. If at any point the duck or goose appears unable to care for her brood, is vicious towards them, has lost interest in or is trampling them (although you might forgive her the odd one), you should remove the youngsters to safety. Don't allow the new family full range until the youngsters are at least a few weeks old,

as they will almost certainly come to harm and are also vulnerable to a wide range of predators, including wild birds.

Rearing without a natural mother

Ducklings and goslings hatched in an incubator will rest for the first day of their lives. Their nutritional needs are taken care of by their utilizing the nourishment from the yolk sac in the egg.

The brooder

Once you have removed them from the hatcher, you will need to put them in a brooder. This can take many forms, the basic requirement being heat. You can rig up a makeshift brooder very quickly, using a cardboard box and a constant heat source such as a radiator or boiler. This type of arrangement can save the lives of youngsters rejected by their mothers or provide overnight care while you sort out something more permanent.

You can buy purpose-made brooders or "electric hens," and if you are hatching a lot this may be a useful purchase. The most usual solution, however, involves some hardboard and a heat lamp.

DIY brooder You can use a dull-emitter ceramic lamp that doesn't emit light and therefore gives the youngsters a natural night, but an infra-red lamp – with a red light, not a bright white one – works well too. Take some hardboard, or similar, and form it into a circle. Make the circle as large or small as you wish, depending on the number of birds you want to rear. The circle must be large enough for the youngsters to get away from the heat source but not so large that they struggle to find it. Then suspend the heat lamp over the middle of the circle or slightly to one side, fixed so that it can be raised gradually as the youngsters get older to reduce the heat. A circle is good because the birds cannot become trapped in a corner and suffocate. You might also wish to be able to

Hatching and Rearing

Above Clean chopped straw is ideal litter for ducklings and goslings.

extend the circle or let the youngsters into the whole of the building as they grow.

Temperature Directly under the lamp the temperature should be 89.6–95°F (32–35°C) and around the lamp 69.8–77°F (21–25°C). However, most breeders don't measure the temperature – they prefer to watch the birds. If they are too hot, they will move as far away from the heat source as possible; if too cold, they huddle together for warmth directly under the lamp. Sticky bottoms are a symptom of being chilled (or being handled roughly).

You must have sufficient lamps for the number of birds. If they can't all get under the lamp, then you need to buy another one or make two pens. It is essential that your heat source is reliable, as the cessation of heat in an outside shed or barn during a cold night will kill the youngsters. Temperatures

plummet at night, so you need to be sure they will be warm enough. If in doubt, use two lamps or keep them in your house for the first few days.

Bedding Provide litter in the form of chopped barley straw or wood shavings, or one of the newer fiber beddings now available. Watch out for goslings eating shavings. Ducklings and goslings are much wetter and messier than chicks, so you will need to clean the brooder frequently, removing any really wet litter and topping off daily with dry litter.

Feeding Provide some green food, especially for goslings. A useful source is to dig up a clump of grass – make sure it is clean and not fouled by domestic animals. Chopped dandelion leaves or lettuce will also be appreciated.

Place starter crumbs away from the heat source. The feed should not become warm, and the young birds need to have some exposure to a slightly cooler area and be encouraged to use their legs. Water, too, should be placed away from the heat source for the same reasons. Use containers that the birds cannot tip over or get into: they must not become soaked, especially in the early days when this could be fatal.

Taming Talk to the youngsters when you feed them, and let them get to know you. But be warned: a gosling or duckling will imprint very strongly on something it comes to regard as "mother." Strike a balance between tameness and dependency. It's good to pick them up and handle them, but remember that they are very young and delicate. Don't let children handle them without supervision or too often.

Outdoors
The next stage is to get the young birds outside on warm days on to good, clean grass. This depends on the weather conditions but should be at about three to four weeks of age, by which time they will be off heat.

The youngsters should still not get wet, must be protected from predators and other birds, and should be penned. They will need a house area as well as a run, which ideally can be moved on to fresh areas. The grass should not have been grazed recently by adult birds, especially for goslings who are prone to picking up gizzard worm (see pages 64–65) which will harm them. They can have a shallow bowl of water but will need to be able to get out of it easily. At this stage they do need to be able to get their heads and necks wet. Now is the time to change the feed gradually to grower pellets: begin by mixing this into the crumbs until they are totally replaced by the new ration.

The aim now is to get the birds outside in their house and run day and night, and as they acclimatize this will become possible. Again, watch out for them getting too cold. If a cold snap occurs, you may have to get them in at night, or even day and night, with a source of heat available.

Becoming adults

As they grow, give the young birds more space and aim to get goslings out on grass. Keep them away from larger grazing animals, as they are still vulnerable since they are not yet fully grown. A special area or nursery paddock would be ideal. Ducklings should be penned and protected until they are large enough to cope – they don't take long to grow to this stage, and commercial breeds will be almost fully grown by seven weeks. You can let your ducklings out of their pen when you are there to supervise them and gently drive them back into their house at night.

Right Goslings do very well on clean, new grass but need protection.

Hatching and Rearing

Change the diet once more. Goslings may get almost all their nutrition from fresh grass in early summer, but otherwise supplement with wheat and provide insoluble grit. Ducks need to move on to an adult ration. All the advice for providing sufficient washing water and, ideally, swimming water for adults (see pages 34–37) applies to these growing birds at this stage.

Ducklings and goslings at markets
If you see ducklings or goslings in down (not feathered up) at markets, especially with no heat source and huddled together, this should ring alarm bells. If you purchase any of these you will need to supply a heat source as quickly as possible, plus they will be very tired. Try to get an accurate hatch date from the seller

and then proceed as for rearing without a mother. The priority is to warm them up. Put the birds in a warm box next to a heat source in the house for the first night, although there should still be a cooler area of the box for them to visit if they become too hot. Feed crumbs and green food to encourage them to eat. You may find that the next day some have sticky material around their vent area from as a result of being chilled. Gently remove this, as if it sticks it can prevent them from passing waste.

Sexing
With ducklings, females make a deep quack and drakes a sort of whistling, higher-pitched quack. Once you hear it, you will easily tell the difference. This

Above Ducklings and goslings need the best start in life, whether they are raised by their mother or by an owner.

Left You have a responsibility for the birds that you have raised – what will you do with surplus male birds?

89

Hatching and Rearing

happens at around five weeks. Apart from the Muscovy, the drake also has a curly tail. Vent sexing is possible but troublesome – you should not try it unless you have an expert to show you how, as it is possible to damage the duckling.

With goslings, vent sexing by an expert is also possible and a few breeds are "auto-sexing" in that the youngsters are different colors according to their sex.

Both drakes and ganders grow bigger than their females. As the birds get older, the male characteristics become more obvious in behavior, plumage, and size. There's not much to be gained for small-scale keepers in knowing the sex early, especially for ducks as they will mature in a matter of weeks and it will become

obvious. But when the sex is known, decisions have to be made on the number of excess males – and there always seem to be more males than females in any hatch! You must not keep more males than females unless you keep the males together, away from the females. Otherwise, you will have to decide what to do with them – and unless they are very good specimens, the answer has to be to grow them on for the table. You are responsible for their welfare, so don't avoid this by sending them to sales for someone else to buy and maybe keep irresponsibly. It is a fact of keeping waterfowl that surplus male birds are simply not required, although they can have a role as pets if there are no females in the vicinity.

Birds on Show

Exhibiting your waterfowl can become an addictive hobby. Not only is there the fun of breeding a bird that is good enough to win, but also the pleasure of meeting up with old friends and like-minded people. This is not an expensive hobby, so why not give it a go?

What is a poultry show?

Poultry shows are competitive exhibitions of the best examples of poultry, including ducks and geese. They developed in the early nineteenth century in the UK and US and initially were purely agricultural, with ducks and geese shown as carcasses.

Development of showing

In an age when transport had been revolutionized by the arrival of the railways and the use of steamships, and with urban development bringing great prosperity for some, collectors in the UK imported what they considered to be exotic breeds from the Empire countries. The Indian Runner duck, for example, caused a great stir with its upright carriage, while breeds with beautiful plumage such as the Black East Indian or Cayuga were highly prized by their owners. This beauty could not be appreciated if the birds were dead, so live breed classes for ducks and geese first appeared in London in 1845. These included Common Goose, Ducks, Cross Aylesbury and Rouen, Asiatic or Knob geese, and Any Other Variety geese and ducks, as well as chickens and turkeys. Collectors in the US were also importing birds via trade routes with Asia as well as from the UK and

Above Ducks at a show with the red cards showing First Place in their various sections.

Left Goose pens are obviously larger than duck pens to allow the goose to move freely.

93

Birds on Show

Europe, and one very early account describes a show that continues today as the Boston Exposition.

Poultry showing was born, and it became necessary to standardize the breeds by compiling descriptions of their characteristics to which exhibitors aspired. It must have been a very exciting time, with new breeds being imported and enthusiasts crossing and selecting to create their own new breeds. The first UK Standards were published in 1865 and included Aylesbury, Rouen, Black East Indian, and Call ducks, plus Embden and Toulouse geese. Other countries followed suit, and the American Poultry Association was formed in 1873.

Showing in the twentieth and twenty-first centuries

Until the middle of the twentieth century, in the UK

exhibitors were able to send birds to shows on the train, labeled for the appropriate classes, and they would be returned at the end of the show with their prizes. Then World War II intervened and showing took a back seat for some years. In 1966/67, the *British Waterfowl Association Yearbook* stated: "This year entries at Shows have been showing a welcome increase and I would hope (in spite of expense and worrying railway problems) that we should increase our number of exhibitors." Amazingly, exhibitions had revived in the UK and elsewhere after the wartime interruption.

Today, although there are perhaps not quite the number of birds exhibited as in the heyday, poultry showing is fast becoming a very popular hobby once again, where competitors can show off their knowledge

Showing worldwide

The mission statement of the South Australian Poultry Association sums up what showing worldwide is all about:

"The South Australian Poultry Association Inc. consists of a number of clubs committed to the promotion of pure breeds of poultry as a vibrant, exciting, and challenging recreational activity that transcends all ages."

and skill at breeding and managing their birds. More recently, poultry shows have picked themselves up from the threat and restrictions of avian flu (see pages 70–71) and learned to adapt to the threat, following new regulations in bio-security.

Modern poultry shows

Today, poultry shows are held either as part of an agricultural show or as specialist shows run by individual poultry clubs. There will be a range of classes, and the way in which they are divided will depend on the size and scope of the show.

Classes

Smaller poultry shows may divide waterfowl into light, medium and heavy ducks and geese and run a class for male and female of each, while bigger shows run classes for individual breeds. Really specialized shows will have classes for the colors of individual breeds such as Runner duck – White and Runner drake – White. Nearly all shows have competitions for children called junior or juvenile classes. Eggs, too, can be shown and may include classes for different colors and for egg contents, where the egg will be broken.

Entries may vary from a hundred or so for a small, local club show to several thousand at one of the big

continental exhibitions, with everything in between. Your first step is to find out the dates of shows in your locality and go along to some before you start showing your own birds.

Show day

The poultry arrive early in the morning and are placed in the pens provided. They should have food and water before being put in the pen for judging, and then again after judging. Competitors then leave the penning area to allow the judges to get on with their task.

A steward or the judge will either take the bird from the pen for assessment or open the pen to examine the bird more closely. The marks or comments will be written down by the steward. In some countries, the birds are simply placed in order of merit; in others, the judge must provide a judging commentary for each bird, justifying its position in the class.

In the UK and US, poultry is usually placed from first to third or lower, but in Europe the practice is for more grading: a bird can be excellent, good, average, below standard, poor, and so on. In this system, all competitors knows exactly what the judge thinks of their bird. Some also believe this system to be preferable to traditional placings since a poor bird can never win a class simply because the rest of the entries are of an even lower standard.

When judging is complete, competitors return to the penning area to find out where they were placed, feed and water their birds, and check the other results. The birds remain on exhibition until "boxing up" at a specified time, when they can be taken home.

A poultry show is a very social experience, with plenty of time to meet up with friends and look at other people's exhibits. There is also always something to learn, however long you have been showing. It is not considered good practice to talk to the judges before they have made their decision, even if you know them, but afterwards you can ask why they placed the birds in the order they did and learn from their answers.

Preparation begins months before the show. In order to do well on the day, you will need to ensure your birds are in the best possible condition and used to being handled by a range of people as well as yourself.

Selecting show stock

The basic requirement for showing at any level is good quality stock. As far as possible, the birds need to meet the Standards that are laid down for their particular breed. Some people exhibit birds they have bought from breeders, while others prefer to show their own stock. Whichever you decide to do, either buy the best or breed the best. The bird will be judged entirely on its adherence to its Breed Standards, so it is pointless taking anything to the show that has obvious faults or inadequacies.

Above A well-presented, well-handled Bali duck proves to be a worthy champion.

Making your entries

However confident you are of the quality of your stock, it is best to start at a smaller show, perhaps a local club event. Read through the schedule and then enter the appropriate classes. Entries often close some weeks in advance to allow organizers to order the correct quantity of penning. Entry fees are usually relatively low, so enter whichever birds you think you will have in good condition at the time of the show and if one is not up to standard on the day simply leave it at home. Some exhibitors enter more birds than they intend to take and make the final selection nearer the time. Don't take too many birds to your first few shows: one or two are quite enough for you to cope with at the beginning.

Preparing your birds

It really helps to "pen tame" your birds – that is, get them used to the type of pen they will be in at the shows, and to having people look at and handle them. It will make it a lot easier for the birds and the judges at the show itself. A bird that is timid or wild may be distressed and could lose feathers and condition.

The birds need to be spotlessly clean for the show. Given the right conditions, geese are naturally clean birds, but make sure that for a day or so before the show they don't get muddy. Reduce grass stains from droppings by taking them off grass 12–24 hours before the show and feeding them pellets. Leave them in their usual house but with plenty of clean, dry bedding. The night before and on the day of the show, check that they are clean underneath. Wash their feet, legs, and bill in warm (not hot), soapy water using a mild, gentle

Above Experienced judges choose their winner – for better of for worse, the judges's decision is final!

soap. An old, soft toothbrush is useful for this. Judges can and will reject birds completely if they have any signs of parasites, so check them over carefully. Do not put the birds in their traveling boxes overnight, as it's not pleasant for them and they will be filthy if you do.

All of this applies to ducks as well, although it is easier to wash their feathered parts if necessary. Rinse in clean water and don't rub the feathers dry as you could damage them.

Going to the show

Gather together a show kit, which should include a bottle of soapy water, a brush, and a towel. Make sure your carry cages are comfortable for the birds and safe so that they won't escape, especially as you will probably have to carry them some distance once you arrive at the show.

Travel to the show should be as stress free as possible, so allow plenty of time. Bear in mind that at the bigger agricultural shows there is likely to be a line to get into the venue. Have your pen numbers or entry details ready when you arrive, so that you can find your pens quickly and install your birds with the minimum of fuss.

After the show

At the end of the day, it is highly likely that you will be tired and so will your birds. Birds like routine and this day will have pushed them well beyond what they consider normal. Take them home as soon as you can and on arrival give them a bowl of water and some food. If you arrive home in the dark, if possible put on a light long enough to allow them to drink and feed before settling down for the night, but don't leave it on as this will keep them awake. Ideally, you should isolate them for a week or so as they will have come into contact with birds from many areas.

Check the birds carefully the following day and keep an eye on them for the next week or so. Then start planning your next show!

Win or lose

If you did not win a prize at the show, be a good loser and learn from it – even if it is simply to avoid that judge in future! You will then be better placed to improve your birds' performance at the next show, and the next...

Join the club

A good way of getting the most from your ducks or geese is to join a local or national poultry or waterfowl club. Even if you don't want to show, membership will offer a number of benefits for you and your birds.

Which club?

Any club is only as good as its members and what they put into it. Poultry and waterfowl clubs are run by volunteers and nearly all could do with a little bit more of the volunteering! This is a great way to get to know other waterfowl keepers and breeders and build up a whole new circle of friends. You will also learn more about your chosen breed through newsletters and regular meetings, and get the opportunity to look at different breeds as well.

You may be lucky enough to have a local club for enthusiasts in your area that includes keepers of all types of poultry and waterfowl. The most active clubs have regular meetings on subjects such as show preparation or a talk from a local feed supplier, plus club-member-only shows and maybe a couple of open shows per year.

There may not always be a club that caters solely for your breed, but you can still join a more generic club such as a goose club. In most countries, the more popular breeds such as Call ducks or Indian Runners have one or more clubs for interested people.

Encompassing all these clubs is the national club for the country, which oversees the Standards and runs the championship shows. Some places have separate waterfowl and poultry clubs that cover the whole of the country. It's interesting, too, to keep an eye on breed clubs and national poultry societies from other countries via newsletters, websites, and shows – sometimes the Standards are a little different, but the enthusiasm and willingness to share experiences and knowledge is the same the world over.

Above A hard-working volunteer organizes the display of information on the Club stand.

Breed Directory

Although all breeds of duck, apart from the Muscovy, have developed from the Mallard, and goose breeds from the Greylag or the Swan goose, they have become distinctive in color and characteristics. Reflecting this is an individual Standard from each country for every breed, representing all that is ideal. The descriptions in this directory follow these Standards, but also provide all the practical information you will need to make the right choice of breed for you.

Call, Bantam, and Miniature breeds

Bantam, miniature (small versions of the larger breeds), and Call ducks are smaller types that are generally good for keeping in gardens and where space is more limited. However, these breeds are also usually capable of flight, and so will need their wings clipped to keep them at home.

Call

alert and attractive • characterful • easy to tame • noisy • poor layer

TYPE: bantam (Call in UK) • WEIGHT: drake 1¼–1½ lb (0.6–0.7 kg), duck 1–1¼ lb (0.5–0.6 kg)
• COLORS: apricot, bibbed, blue fawn, dark silver, magpie, mallard, pied, silver, white, plus non-standard colors including dusky, butterscotch, black, with others in development

Duck Breeds

This delightful little duck has a huge following. With its alert eyes, "busy" personality, and willingness to be tamed, the Call duck is instantly appealing and consequently very popular. It is therefore quite easy to obtain, although buying exhibition standard birds is much more difficult. If you want to breed or show, you will need to visit the best breeders and explain your requirements.

The original name of Dutch Call ducks gives some indication of the breed's origin: in Holland they are rather aptly referred to as *Kwakers* and, in turn, believed to have originated in Asia. The Dutch were great seafarers and a colonial power – Indonesia was known as the Dutch East Indies until the late 1940s – so ducks were no doubt part of the goods and livestock traded throughout the world. It is known that the birds were in England before 1851 and the US before 1884. Also originally known as Decoy ducks (*de Kooi* = a trap), they were used to encourage wildfowl into traps on lakes, a method documented since the seventeenth century in Holland and widely employed in the eighteenth and nineteenth centuries in the UK. As Dutch engineers drained large areas of eastern England in the late seventeenth and early eighteenth centuries, they no doubt realized the potential use in the Fenland for these little birds.

For such a widespread bird, Call ducks faded dramatically during the twentieth century right up until the 1970s. Their use as a Decoy duck had more or less come to an end,

Khaki Call drake

White Call duck

with the vast wetlands used for wildfowling now tamed and in use for agriculture. A population immersed in fighting two World Wars and rationed on food no doubt saw little use for a small duck with limited egg-laying ability.

From the 1970s on, breeders and duck keepers began to take an interest in Call ducks once again. With their great personality, beautiful colors, and small size, their popularity grew to a point where now there are often more entries in their classes at poultry and waterfowl shows than in any other. They are particularly suitable for children and the junior or juvenile classes at shows often feature Call ducks, which can be handled and tamed easily by their young owners.

Looks

The breed has been compared to a "bathtub duck" and indeed they do resemble the type of plastic duck you might float in your bath water, with their large, appealing eyes and round face. The range of colors is astounding and the plumage is fascinating. In the silver, for example, the drake's back is described as "light gray with black frosting, shading to black with beetle-green sheen on the rump." However, for many enthusiasts the white Call duck – which at its best is the purest of pure white – is the most striking.

Personality

The Call duck has a bubbly, open personality and is alert and interested in everything. It does not go by that name for no reason, because it is very noisy with a really loud and persistent quack. Therefore, perhaps a Call duck is not to be recommended if you have neighbors close by.

Uses

Call ducks are ideal for new duck keepers, and because they are popular there are lots of clubs and societies to provide help and advice. They are not great egg layers, so their main use is as pets or exhibition birds for all ages. Because they call out at any visitor, they also make good alarm birds.

Day to day

Call ducks bond more closely in their pairs or trios than other ducks and a breeding trio would be a good purchase. If you split up established pairs or trios, they will become very distressed. The Call ducklings are especially vulnerable to predators of all kinds due to their diminutive size.

Providing swimming water is easy, as these little ducks will be happy with a small, portable pond. Because of their small feet and light weight, they don't paddle the ground and turn it into mud as quickly as the larger breeds. Good management and appropriate stocking will ensure they won't damage the ground at all. Call ducks can fly well, so you will need to clip their wings.

Gray Call drake

Counterclockwise: Blue-bibbed Call, Magpie Call and the head of a Khaki Call

Duck Breeds

Black East Indian

spectacular plumage • hardy • can be timid • poor layer • difficult breeder

TYPE: **bantam** • WEIGHT: **drake 2 lb (0.9 kg), duck 1½–1¾ lb (0.7–0.8 kg)** • COLOR: **black**

This duck is also known as the Labrador, Black East Indie, East Indie, Black Brazilian, and Buenos Aires. Despite these names, it is generally agreed that the breed originated in the US, although some have theorized that it arose in the Punjab. In his 1990 book *The East Indie Duck*, the American breeder and judge Darrel Sheraw concluded: "There is no breed of domestic duck whose origin is so shrouded in mystery as that of the East Indie." It was first documented in the US in the early nineteenth century and in the UK from the 1830s, so the breed is well established. Some believe it is a sport from a Mallard and it does indeed resemble the latter more than a Call duck type – perhaps this is why the flesh is often described as gamey.

Looks

The striking black plumage with its glossy, beetle-green sheen makes the Black East Indian unforgettable. It should not have any white feathers: when buying, check under the throat where a small patch may be hidden. The green sheen should be intense, while the underside of the wings will be a solid black color. The bill and legs, too, are black and the eyes dark brown. As females age they tend to produce some white feathers which increase year by year, and an older male may show white circles around the eyes. The aim, though, is for solid color, and this should certainly be the standard in young and breeding birds.

Personality

This very hardy duck is a good flyer so you will need to clip its wings, especially as it can be quickly startled into flight. It is quite a shy bird so don't expect to tame it too easily, although this will depend on the strain. Some consider the Black East Indian to be halfway between a wildfowl and a domestic duck, although it is classified as a domestic.

Uses

This is an impressive exhibition bird and very ornamental. It is not a prolific egg layer and can be difficult to breed. The first eggs may be covered in a distinctive charcoal-colored or even black deposit which can be scraped away, but later clutches will be a dull white.

Day to day

The Black East Indian needs to keep active and enjoys access to water. The better its condition, the more impressive the black/green sheen. The birds are best kept as a trio or pair if you wish to breed from them.

These ducks clearly show the intense green sheen of the plumage.

Black East Indian male

Crested Miniature

"pom-pom" crest • active and agile • enjoys foraging • good layer • difficult breeder

TYPE: **miniature** • WEIGHT: **drake 2½ lb (1.1 kg), duck 2 lb (0.9 kg)** • COLORS: **white, colored**

A replica of the large Crested ducks, the Crested Miniature is a relatively recent creation, first bred by Roy Sutcliffe in Yorkshire in the late 1980s. The first pair were seen in public at the 1992 Rare Breeds Survival Trust Show and Sale and sold for over $200 (£100). Its first show category was at the British Waterfowl Association National Show in 1994, and the breed Standard was laid down in 1997.

Looks

When moving, this little duck is fairly upright at an angle of around 35–40°, but the characteristic that really draws the eye is the crest on the head. Consisting of a small mass of fatty tissue from which the feathers grow, it is often described as a "topknot" or "pom-pom" and should be round and prominent. It sits up on the center of the head, not over the eyes, and the feathering should be tight so that the crest is dense. There is, however, plenty of room for error and crests do vary in size, shape, and even placement. All colors are permissible as long as the markings are symmetrical, so there is a range of different combinations. In the white version, the legs and feet should be orange and the bill orange-yellow, which is very striking against the white base.

Personality

This is an active little bird that enjoys foraging. You have to watch out for the size of the crest. If it's too big it will get dirty on range and you may need to trim it – which is not acceptable if you are planning to exhibit.

Uses

A lovely exhibition bird, the Crested Miniature is also surprisingly useful as it can lay up to 100 eggs per year.

Day to day

This bird is not an easy breeder. It is even more difficult to produce a good crest, and there are usually some plain-headed offspring as well. Watch out for the drake getting hold of the crest during mating and damaging the duck. The crest itself will lose feathers anyway, so a breeding duck cannot be exhibited. The drake is usually very active.

Crested Miniature male

Crested Miniature female

Silver Appleyard Miniature

very ornamental • compact • hardy • good layer • easy breeder

TYPE: **miniature** • WEIGHT: **drake 3 lb (1.4 kg), duck 2½ lb (1.1 kg)** • COLOR: **silver**

A small replica of the large Silver Appleyard, this miniature was bred by well-known American waterfowl breeder Tom Bartlett in 1980 and rapidly became very popular. There was some confusion between these and the original bantam ducks that were created by Reginald Appleyard, which are now called the Silver Bantam duck (see page 112). The two breeds have been standardized separately.

Looks

The Standard is very precise, but in summary: the drake has a black-green head with a silver-white flecked throat encircled by a silver-white ring. The base of the neck is claret fading to silver under the body, with the back ranging from laced claret near the head down to dark gray with a solid black-green rump. His wings have blue tips. The duck is no less interesting, with a silver-white head and neck, the crown of the head and back of the neck fawn continuing along the back, and the underbody creamy white. She, too, has blue-tipped wings, which makes these an exceptionally handsome couple.

Personality

Exceptionally pretty and eye-catching, this breed is also extremely vigorous and hardy.

Uses

The Silver Appleyard Miniature is a very good layer. Despite its small size, it is a compact and meaty bird that is good for the table. This breed is also perfect for exhibition, its diminutive stature making it easy to handle.

Day to day

If you don't want the birds to keep breeding and you want eggs, you'll have to collect the eggs regularly and prevent them from sitting, as this bird is an easy breeder. It is a challenge to breed an exhibition bird with just the right markings, but take care to select for the compact shape as well as color.

An eyecatching and hardy female duck.

Silver Appleyard Miniature male and female

Silver Bantam

beautiful color • placid • slightly erect when moving • hardy • good layer

TYPE: **bantam** • WEIGHT: **drake 2 lb (0.9 kg), duck 1¾ lb (0.8 kg)** • COLOR: **silver**

Duck Breeds

This duck was developed in Suffolk by Reginald Appleyard, a very famous breeder in the 1940s, who was aiming for utility performance. It was thought to be the small version of his famous large duck, the Silver Appleyard, but was not – hence the confusion between this breed and Silver Appleyard Miniature (see page 110) which was developed later. It is thought that the breed arose by crossing a white Call drake with a small Khaki Campbell duck, and it first appeared in the Standards in 1982 as the Silver Appleyard Bantam. Because of the popularity of the Miniature, which is a little larger, the Silver Bantam is now more difficult to find, especially in its correct form.

Looks

The Standard is very precise, but in summary: the drake has a black head and neck with a green sheen. The breast and shoulders are red-brown with white lacing; the belly, flank, and stern are silver-white. The back is gray with black stippling. The duck's head and neck are fawn with graining in dark brown or black. The breast is cream, the shoulders have brown streaks and she is cream underneath. The rump is fawn-gray with brown flecks. In both sexes, the eyes are dark brown and the legs orange.

Personality

A hardy, healthy bird; calm and easy to tame.

Uses

This duck is a good layer if you collect the eggs regularly. It also looks good on the show bench.

Day to day

This duck is a good sitter and likes to raise young. However, it is very difficult to breed a Silver Bantam with the correct color and markings – there is a tendency for ducks to be far too pale, which is a major

Silver Bantam female and male

Australian Spotted

delightful plumage • strong personality • calm • active flyer and forager • good layer

TYPE: bantam • WEIGHT: drake 2¼ lb (1 kg), duck 2 lb (0.9 kg) • COLORS: greenhead, bluehead, silverhead

Despite what its name implies, this breed originated in the US where it was developed in the 1920s by John C. Kriner and Stanley Mason of Pennsylvania. It was bred from Call ducks, Mallards, Northern Pintails, and an unidentified Australian duck breed. It became better known to the public in the 1990s but overall numbers are still not high, which is a shame considering its great beauty.

Looks

This duck carries itself almost horizontal due to the legs being set on centrally. The color is very complex, but in brief: the drake's head can be green (greenhead), blue (bluehead), or silver (silverhead). The neck has a white band and the sides of the body and breast are deep burgundy, with the center of the breast and the underbody white. The shoulders and back are dark gray. In the duck, the greenhead's body, head and neck are fawn spotted with dark brown. In the bluehead and silverhead, these spots are bluish gray and silver respectively.

Personality

These ducks have plenty of personality and are very calm. They are active flyers so you will need to clip their wings.

Uses

Australian Spotted ducks are excellent layers and can produce up to 125 cream, blue, or green eggs per year. They are also efficient at reducing garden pests and also for removing mosquito larvae from pools.

Day to day

These ducks love to forage so you will need to provide them with the space to do so. They make very good mothers and the breed matures fast, with drakes showing male behavior at only four to five weeks old.

Duck Breeds

A female Australian Spotted silverhead

Light duck breeds

Some of the best egg layers fall within this classification. Ducks were actively bred for eggs during the first half of the twentieth century, with some impressive results. Indian Runners come into this category and it is partly due to their laying record that people first realized ducks had the ability to lay well, in addition to being tough, hardy birds.

Abacot Ranger

prominent hood • active • good forager • hardy • good layer • poor flyer

TYPE: **light** • WEIGHT: drake 5½–6 lb (2.5–2.7 kg), duck 5–5½ lb (2.3–2.5 kg) • COLORS: combination, including red-brown and fawn-gray

Duck Breeds

The Abacot Ranger was developed by Oscar Grey of Friday Wood near Colchester, Essex, between 1917 and 1923 and named Abacot after his premises. (Interestingly, Abacot has come to mean a form of ancient cap worn by kings, although this was a misspelled version of the original old French word *bycoket*.) Mr. Grey was aiming to produce a utility bird – a good egg layer with an acceptable carcass – and he certainly succeeded. The bird was bred from white "sports" from purebred Khaki Campbells and white Indian Runner drakes. There was a fashion during World War I of naming new breeds with military terms, so its original name was the Hooded Ranger duck in both the US and UK.

The breed was introduced into Germany in the early 1920s and standardized in 1934 as the *Streicher-Ente* (Ranger duck). It fell out of favor in the UK from the

An Abacot Ranger drake

end of the 1920s, but continued successfully in Germany with only minor differences. In 1980, the breed made a return to the UK through the interest of keen waterfowl fanciers who imported some eggs. The current standards used in the UK are a translation of the German standards, as these are very close to the original ideal of the breeder.

Looks

The hood of both sexes is a prominent feature. In drakes, the head and neck are brown-black with a green sheen, circled by a silver neck ring, while in ducks the head and neck are fawny buff with the top of the head strongly grained in dark brown (not black). The drake's breast and shoulder are a rich red-brown and his belly, flanks, and stern are silvery white to cream. The female's breast is particularly attractive, being lightly streaked with light brown on a pale cream background. The bills of the sexes are different: the drake's is yellowish green and the female's dark gray, almost black. As the bill is colored up by the time the birds are eight weeks old, it makes a useful and accurate guide for determining their sex.

Personality

This bird carries itself slightly erect and is active, alert, and busy. It rarely flies.

The hood and neck ring are both promient features of the Abacot Ranger.

Uses

The Abacot Ranger makes a striking exhibition bird but, having been bred originally as a utility duck, it is also a very useful egg layer, producing up to 250 eggs per year.

Day to day

It is an enthusiastic forager, and given a decent range the Abacot Ranger can find a good proportion of its own food. The Abacot Ranger is capable of rearing young and can make a good mother.

Bali

small, round crest • Indian Runner shape • active forager • good layer • difficult to breed

TYPE: light • WEIGHT: 5 lb (2.3 kg), duck 4 lb (1.8 kg) • COLORS: white, colored

The Bali originated where the name suggests and is indigenous to this Indonesian island lying to the west of Java. Ancient stone carvings depict the typically upright duck, which indicate it has been in existance for many years. The duck is still very much part of Bali life: travelers remark on the spectacle of the ducks being led out to the paddy fields, where they eat the pests that damage the rice, and also seeing them waiting to be led back at night. The Bali duck was introduced to the UK in 1925 from Malaysia by the Misses Davidson and Chisolm, keen Indian Runner breeders. It was standardized in 1930. It later all but disappeared until the 1980s and is still an unusual duck in both the UK and US — but it is a great choice for exhibition, which no doubt fueled its revival.

Looks

To the untrained eye, the Bali looks like a white Indian Runner with a crest, but it is actually a little heavier. The orange legs are strong and set well back, and the little round crest sits on the back of the

A white Bali

head. The eyes are blue and the bill orange-yellow. Mainly seen in white, all other colors are permissible as long as the markings are symmetrical.

Personality
This is an active duck that is a good forager and easy to drive to a foraging area, as it flocks well. It is a poor flyer.

Uses
The Bali is a good egg layer, producing anything between 100 and 200 eggs per year, depending on the strain. It is also good for controlling pests in the garden.

Day to day
All crested ducks are difficult to breed, throwing a proportion of plain-headed youngstock and an abnormally high number of dead-in-shell. This can be distressing for a beginner, so if you want to take up this breed seriously you will need to understand some basic genetics in order to be successful. Waterfowl and breed clubs can help you to achieve the best hatch by explaining the genetics behind breeding problems.

Bali ducks are most commonly white, but do exist in other colors.

Campbell

super-high layer • placid • excellent forager • easy to raise artificially • non-flyer

TYPE: light • WEIGHT: drake 5–5½ lb (2.3–2.5 kg), duck in laying condition 4½–5 lb (2–2.3 kg) • COLORS: khaki, white, dark

This breed was developed by Mrs. Adele Campbell and is said to have begun its existence in her orchard at Uley, Gloucestershire, in 1901. According to Mrs. Campbell, it started as a result of mating an Indian Runner duck, the highest egg layer at the time, with a Rouen drake. Other influences such as Mallard and fawn-and-white Runners were later introduced to form the Khaki Campbell. The British were fighting the Boer War at the time, so naming the breed Khaki Campbell was a patriotic gesture. The breed standard was not very precise, as it was the utility – egg-laying – that was prized. The Khaki Campbell was standardized in the US in 1941.

The White Campbell was developed by Captain F. S. Pardoe in 1924, although it wasn't standardized until the 1950s. It was very important to the breeder that the bird retained the utility characteristics of its Khaki counterpart. H. R. S. Humphreys is credited with developing the Dark Campbell, its existence being announced in 1943. The purpose of this color was for sex linkage,

since Mr. Humphreys was keen on auto-sexing breeds (where the sexes of the ducklings can be determined by the color on hatching). In this case, the darker-colored ducklings were drakes. Perhaps because auto-sexing was not as desirable in ducks as in chickens, due to their rapid growth and the fact that the drakes could be destined for the table, this breed color did not really catch on and is

now quite difficult to breed and throws up faults due to the small gene pool.

However, writing in *Poultry and Poultry Husbandry* in 1933, breeder Charles Roscoe said: "It will pay to keep the so-called White Campbell or the genuine Khaki Campbell. The drakes from the White Campbells may produce 1s 3d profit on their sale as table birds as against no profit on the sale of the real Khaki Campbell... I believe that the best proposition is to keep Khaki Campbells for laying

A Kahki Campbell

Male and female dark Campbell

and learn to sex the ducklings at day-olds and sell off the drakelets for what one can get for them." Presumably the market preferred the White table bird and for a time there was a real demand to be able to sex ducklings in the other colors at hatching.

Looks

The carriage of the Campbell is midway between a Runner type and a heavy table bird, with the stance slightly upright. The Khaki drake has a green-bronze head, neck, rump and secondaries (visible wing feathers), and the rest of the body is an even, warm khaki shading to lighter khaki towards the lower part of the breast. The bill is a dark greenish blue and the legs are dark orange. The duck is an even shade of warm khaki, darker around the head and neck. The bill is dark slate with the legs as close to the body shade as possible.

White is, of course, pure white all over with orange legs and bill and gray-blue eyes. The Dark Campbell drake has a beetle-green head and neck, and a light brown body with dark gray-brown penciling on the feathers, gradually shading to gray towards the rear of the bird. The primaries (flight feathers) on the wings are dark brown and the tail is dark gray-brown with beetle-green coverts (covering feathers). Legs are bright orange and his bill bluish green.

The duck is dark brown on the head and neck and light brown over the shoulders, breast, and flank, with each feather broadly penciled in dark brown. The back and tail are dark brown and the rump beetle-green. Her legs are as near her body color as possible and her bill is a slatey brown.

Personality

An excellent forager, the Campbell loves to look for insects. The temperament is placid enough for you to keep a few ducks with your hens, and they do not fly. They do not necessarily need swimming water, but they love to splash so tubs are important.

Uses

They will produce a phenomenal number of eggs – 300 plus per year is not unusual, comparable to the best chickens. They are also good birds for the table.

Day to day

Campbells need to be fed well in addition to foraging actively. They were developed not to be sitters and do not like to go broody: if they do sit, they may keep it up for only a matter of hours or days. There is therefore no need to keep them as breeding trios or pairs. Drakes are very active, so severely limit the number in relation to females. Campbells are quite messy birds so don't overstock.

Pair of dark Campbell ducks

Female Khaki Campbell

Crested

globular crest • ornamental • confident and alert • good layer • difficult breeder

TYPE: **light** • WEIGHT: **drake 7 lb (3.2 kg), duck 6 lb (2.7 kg)** • COLORS: **white, colored**

Duck Breeds

Known as Tufta in some countries, the origin of this duck is not clear: it was depicted in seventeenth-century Dutch paintings yet was well known in the UK in Victorian times. In *Ducks and Geese and How to Keep Them*, which was first published in 1924, F. J. S. Chatterton stated that "it has been bred more on the Continent than in this country [the UK] and there is reason to believe it originated in Holland," and says of the head that "it has the distinguishing characteristic of a ball-shaped crest on the head, which reminds one of the crest on the head of a Polish fowl...". Whatever its beginnings, the Crested duck is popular today not only for its attractive appearance but also because it is a consistent egg layer that is large enough for the table.

Looks

The crest can vary considerably, but ideally should be round and tightly feathered, set in the center of the head and not over the eyes or slipping to one side. The feathers grow into a mass of fatty tissue that comes up through a gap in the skull. A drake will pull feathers out of the duck's crest during mating, but watch out for him causing her pain and damage by getting hold of the tissue as well. The white Crested is pure white with an orange-yellow bill and orange legs, and blue eyes. Any other color is also acceptable, but to win prizes in the show pen the markings must be symmetrical.

Personality

This duck is a confident character and very alert. Despite the pretty crest, it is a good forager.

Uses

The Crested duck is a lovely bird to exhibit. It can also produce up to 100 (sometimes even more) good-sized eggs per year.

Day to day

Take care that the crest does not become clogged with mud or waste food, or become caught up on wire, for example. Clean washing water for the head and neck is essential all year round. As with all crested ducks, it is not easy to breed due to the associated genetic problems, so seek advice from waterfowl or breed clubs.

Crested ducks come in a variety of colors.

Pair of white Crested ducks

Hook Bill

distinctive appearance • good forager • dual purpose • good flyer

TYPE: light • WEIGHT: drake 7 lb (3.2 kg), duck 6 lb (2.7 kg) • COLORS: white, dark Mallard

Duck Breeds

This very old breed was first documented in the seventeenth century. Although it is thought to have originated in Asia, it has long been associated with the canals of Holland, where it was kept intensively for eggs. It was left more or less to fend for itself, flying off to find food and returning in the evening. There are theories that the bill – which is curved in a semi circle, pointing downwards – was developed deliberately so that the wildfowlers could tell the difference between this domestic duck and the wild Mallard. In the UK it had a difficult history and became very rare, kept only by the most dedicated enthusiasts. As with so many other breeds, the Hook Bill was picked up again in the late 1980s but it still remains a minority breed, which is a shame as it is so distinctive.

Looks

This duck carries itself quite erect and when viewed from the side the upper neck, head, and long bill are strongly curved in a semi-circle. It is standardized in three colors. The white is a

pure white with a white or flesh-colored bill and bright orange legs. The dark Mallard is an attractive bird: the drake has an emerald-green head and neck, changing to dark green on the lower neck and clearly cut from the breast which is steel-blue. The flanks and stern are steel-blue while the back is ash color on top with green reflections and the rump green. On the wings,

Non-standardized Hook Bill drake

the primaries (flight feathers) are dark brown-gray and the secondaries (visible wing feathers) dull brown; other feathering on the wing area is a dark slate-blue with some areas showing penciling. The

Non-standardized female

duck is marked in a similar way. The white-bibbed dark Mallard is the same as the dark Mallard except for a white, heart-shaped bib on the lower neck and breast which renders this variation particularly striking to look at.

Personality
The Hook Bill is a good forager, and is light enough to fly so you will need to clip its wings.

Uses
This breed lays 100-plus eggs per year and makes a good table bird.

Day to day
The duck likes to brood her own eggs, so Hook Bills are best kept as breeding trios or pairs. Incubating eggs artificially is not particularly successful.

Indian Runner

very upright • active • prefers ranging to swimming • flocks well • good layer

TYPE: light • WEIGHT: drake 3½–5 lb (1.6–2.3 kg), duck 3–4½ lb (1.4–2 kg) • COLORS: huge range, many standardized including American fawn-and-white, Mallard, trout-and-white

Duck Breeds

This striking breed has had a huge influence on many others and was considered the outstanding egg layer prior to the development of the truly great breeds such as the Khaki Campbell. In his 1918 publication *Runner Ducks*, E. A. Taylor – originator of the now defunct Utility Duck Club – claimed that "the Indian Runner may be termed the 'egg' and land duck *par excellence*. It is built on light, mobile lines in order to range far afield in search of its own food, its activity enables it to cover a surprising amount of ground. With head and neck extended and eye like a hawk's, it actually prefers racing over the land to idling on a pond."

The breed originates from the East Indies and there are stone carvings in Java that may date it to 2,000 years old or even more. The name Indian Runner was coined since prior to the twentieth century it was generally thought that the breed came from India – probably due to a confusion with names and countries at the time of importation (early importers referred to them as "penguin" ducks because of their

Pair of Saxony Indian Runners

stance and shape). The ducks traveled a long way from their native home in the Indonesian islands and Malaya, yet they survived and were often back in lay just weeks later. As early as 1876 there was a class for fawn Runners at the Dumfries Show in Scotland.

Published in 1908, *Utility Poultry Farming for Australasia* – "the book for the man with 6 birds or 6,000" – noted that the Indian Runner was known as the "Leghorn of Duckdom" and said that it was "far too well known in Australasia to need much comment." J. B. Merrett (editor of the *New Zealand Poultry Journal*), who revised the book, believed that where conditions were not suitable for hens the farmer should adopt this breed of duck for producing eggs at low cost.

Duck keepers in the UK were equally convinced, with E. A. Taylor stating that: "The future of the Runner is assured... In the near future when its value is fully known to farmers, Smallholders and all interested in egg-production, it will be stocked in preference to the hen." That commercial future never quite materialized, although many smallholders and farmers did well from selling duck eggs during both World Wars. Despite this absence of success, the Indian Runner has not lost popularity and is enjoyed worldwide by the modern generation of farmers, pet duck keepers, and exhibitors.

White Indian Runner

Looks

This breed has been compared to a hock bottle in shape, and the Indian Runner Club of Great Britain says that "a duck that cannot maintain a natural carriage of at least 40 degrees to the horizontal will not be considered a pure Runner." According to the British Waterfowl Standards, 1999, when not startled – in which case the bird becomes almost perpendicular – or when moving, the body may be inclined between 50 and 80 degrees above the horizontal.

The Indian Runner comes in a wide variety of colors; many are standardized, but breeders are continually developing more with a view to standardizing them in the future. The head is described as lean and racy looking; the neck is long, slender, and in line with the body which is long, narrow, and cylindrical. The legs are set back to allow the upright stance and it is very important that the bird has tight feathering.

Personality

This duck does not fly but ranges over a large area. It does not need swimming water, just enough for splashing over its head and neck. It flocks well, making it easy to move from place to place – Indian

An Indian Runner's head is lean and racy looking.

Runners are sometimes seen in place of sheep at sheepdog demonstrations.

Uses

This is a very rewarding duck to keep for eggs, for beauty, and for foraging.

Older books claim that it lays up to 300 eggs per year, but these days 150–200 is the average. The Indian Runner is such an excellent pest controller and (for a duck) light on its feet, that it truly is the gardener's friend. There are plenty of clubs and associations that can help you get started with the breed.

Day to day

Generally, this duck is not a good sitter, so it is best to incubate the eggs artificially. The slender females are easily injured by a persistent drake's attentions, so it's essential to have a low ratio of drakes to ducks and to remove the drake or the duck if problems arise. Drakes on their own make useful pets and/or foragers, since they rarely fight.

Pair of non-standardized Runners

Magpie

strikingly marked • alert • excellent forager • poor flyer • good layer

TYPE: light • WEIGHT: drake 5½–7 lb (2.5–3.2 kg), duck 4½–6 lb (2–2.7 kg) • COLORS: predominantly black-and-white, also blue-and-white, dun-and-white

Duck Breeds

This breed originates from west Wales, where it had been seen living on small farms for some years before Oliver Drake and M. C. Gower-Williams brought it to the public's attention and developed the breed during the early 1920s. By 1941 Charles Roscoe had a section on the breed in his book *Ducks and Duck Keeping* in a chapter on "The Breed of Duck to Keep." Even at this time he was conceding that "it requires skill to produce birds that are accurately marked."

The breed fell out of favor during the 1950s, but by the early 1980s poultry exhibitors had picked it up again, although only in the black-and-white form. Isaac Hunter of Michigan imported Magpies into the US in 1963 and the American Poultry Association recognized the breed in 1977. They are currently considered a rare breed.

Two further colors – the blue-and-white and the dun-and-white – were standardized in the UK by 1997, although the blue-and-white had been documented since the mid-1920s.

Looks

The Magpie has a strong body that carries at around 35 degrees when active. The color markings are particularly important. For all the colors, the markings should be as close to the following ideal as possible: the head and neck show a black cap covering the whole of the crown to the top of the eyes. The breast and underbody are white. The back of the body is solid black from the shoulders to the tip of the tail. When viewing the duck with closed wings, there should appear to be a heart shape of color over the back. The bill should be yellow, but in older birds the drake's may become spotted with green and the duck's may be gray-green. The legs are orange. Additional colors such as chocolate-and-white and lavender-and-white are available in Europe.

Personality

This duck is alert and a first-rate forager. Although not technically capable of sustained flight, if scared it can get over low heights. Some breeders feel Magpies are quite highly strung.

Uses

This duck is a good layer, producing 200-plus mainly white but sometimes blue or green eggs per year. It is also suitable for the table. Otherwise, the Magpie makes a good pet.

Day to day

Magpies are straightforward to keep. Although they breed easily, to produce a well-marked bird is a great challenge. The advantage is that if you are serious about breeding, you can see very early on which ducklings have good markings. It is well worth taking time to study the basic genetics before attempting to breed as it will help you to understand how to achieve success with your breeding program. More experienced Magpie breeders are normally happy to explain.

Magpie trio

134 Orpington

energetic • alert and intelligent • good backyard bird • rarely flies • dual purpose

TYPE: light • WEIGHT: drake 5–7½ lb (2.3–3.4 kg), duck 5–7lb (2.3–3.2 kg) • COLOR: buff

William Cook, who bred the Orpington chicken in the town of the same name in Kent, also developed the Orpington duck. He began advertising them as buff Orpington ducks in the poultry press from 1910 onwards. The origins of the breed are thought to lie in the crossing and selection of

Orpington female

Aylesbury, Rouen, Cayuga, and Indian Runner parents.

Although never able to compete with the Khaki Campbell as an egg layer, the Orpington was a respectable layer and its advantage was that it was heavier, making it a more attractive dual-purpose egg and table bird. In *Duck Keeping for Pleasure and Profit*, published in 1946, V. Birtwhistle is enthusiastic about the duck, stating that "the Buff is a general purpose bird, combining beauty with table qualities and profitable egg production." It's a statement that small-scale duck keepers could still make today.

The Orpington is an attractive breed to exhibit and has a strong following. Some people like to keep both the hens and the ducks on their land, although these days the duck is usually the better layer.

Looks

This breed should not have upright carriage and has a long, broad, and deep body with strong legs. The drake shows an even shade of buff, and the head and neck are

brown and glossy but with no hint of green. The duck is a rich, even shade of buff throughout and both sexes have brown eyes and orange-red legs.

Personality

These are energetic birds, alert and intelligent. They rarely fly and will adapt well to living in a backyard situation.

Uses

The Orpington is a good layer, producing up to 200 large white eggs per year. It is also suitable for the table.

Day to day

Orpingtons enjoy swimming water but will thrive very well without, although they will need something to splash in. They do well penned (but not if overstocked) or free range, and are comparatively easy to breed.

Orpington trio

Pomeranian (Pommern)

calm • good forager • hardy • moderate layer • fast growing for the table

TYPE: light • WEIGHT: drake 6¾ lb (3 kg), duck 5½ lb (2.5 kg) • COLORS: black, blue

This attractive duck was developed from birds reared on local farms in the Pomerania district in north-eastern Europe, on the German/Swiss border. They have been mentioned as pure breeds since the 1920s.

Although it is often mistaken for the Blue Swedish, the Pomeranian is actually slightly smaller in stature. The Shetland is another similar blue duck, leading to speculation that all the blue-colored breeds share a common origin in the coastal areas of Sweden, Germany, and Holland.

Looks

This breed has a broad and deep, fairly long body and carries itself horizontally. Although it does not look plump, it is quite solid. There are two recognized colors: the blue is an attractive bird and should be an even, light blue sporting a white bib on the upper breast, while the black has the same markings with a green sheen.

Personality

These birds are good foragers and are very hardy. Although active, they have a calm disposition.

Uses

This is a good dual-purpose duck. It will lay around 150 white or bluish-green eggs per year and is quick to mature for the table.

Day to day

As they are good foragers, they do need access to some range and do not do so well confined to a run.

Pomeranian male and female

Overberg

colorful, silky plumage • calm • dual purpose • easy breeder

TYPE: light • WEIGHT: drake 5–5½ lb (2.3–2.5 kg), duck 4½–5 lb (2–2.3 kg) • COLORS: drake a mixture of lilac-blue, brown and cream, duck yellowy brown and cream

The Dutch-sounding name reflects the genesis of this breed, which was through selective breeding in Holland. The parents probably included Abacot Ranger, Hook Bill, and Welsh Harlequin stock.

Looks

This duck moves slightly upright and does not waddle. It has a well-rounded head with an almost straight bill. The body is rounded and medium in length, with strong legs set well underneath it. The plumage is very sleek. The drake's head and neck are pale lilac-blue with a slight brown overlay extending to the wide, white ring encircling the neck. The breast and flank are rich mahogany-brown with white lacing, while the rump and tail are lilac-blue bordered with cream. Underneath, the drake is creamy white except under the tail, where he is lilac-blue. He has a pale lilac-blue speculum (back part of the wing feathers) with a browny yellow overlay and his legs are bright orange. The duck has a yellowy brown head tinged with bluey brown at the top. The back is a pale yellow as are the breast and flanks, changing to a dark cream towards the belly. The belly is pale yellow to cream and the legs are dark dun.

Personality

The Overberg is active and alert, yet has a calm and pleasant disposition.

Uses

This duck was developed to be a good layer of between 170 and 200 eggs per year, as well as to produce a meaty carcass. In addition it is very decorative, being likened by some to a bluish version of the Welsh Harlequin (see page 138).

Day to day

This duck is an easy breeder and is more than capable of raising its own brood.

Overberg male and female

Duck Breeds

Welsh Harlequin

calm • poor flyer • dual purpose • easy breeder

TYPE: light • WEIGHT: drake 5–5½ lb (2.3–2.5 kg), duck 4½–5 lb (2–2.3 kg) • COLOR: harlequin effect

Duck Breeds

This breed was developed by Group Captain Leslie Bonnet in the late1940s from Khaki Campbell "sports," although he later crossed these with other breeds. This took place in Hertfordshire, but the family moved to North Wales and continued with the breed, at which point they were named Welsh Harlequin. In 1968 the flock was decimated by a fox when they were not shut in properly, and the Group Captain lost the birds that were descended from his original two sports. Amazingly, in 1963 a Mr. Eddie Grayson of Lancashire had bought some of the original Welsh Harlequins from the Group Captain, whom he very much admired, and he still had them. He wrote and promoted a Standard and formed a club for the breed, which was imported into the US in 1968. The Standard was accepted in 1987, leading to more interest in this breed with the delightful name.

Looks

The drake has a green and bronze head with a white ring around the neck. The breast and shoulders are a rich red-brown mahogany laced with white, and the underbody is creamy white. There is a tortoiseshell effect on the wings and the legs are orange. The duck has a honey-fawn head and neck, while her main body is fawn to cream with a mid-brown rump. The lacing on her wings, too, gives a pleasing tortoiseshell effect.

Personality

A docile and placid breed, the Welsh Harlequin doesn't fly well and is happy to stay on the farm or in the garden.

Uses

This is a dual-purpose bird. Egg laying varies according to strain: the top end is around 200 per year, but 100–150 is more usual. The breed is also big enough for the table.

Day to day

Welsh Harlequins will raise their own brood. Do not keep too many drakes to ducks, as the males have a high libido and will damage the females.

Welsh Harlequin female

Welsh Harlequin males

Heavy duck breeds

While the light breeds include the best layers, the heavy breeds were developed largely for the table and prized for their ability to convert food into weight. The desire to breed for eggs came after the interest in breeding for meat, and this classification includes some breeds that have been used for food worldwide for many centuries. They are less active than the lightweight ducks, yet these breeds really do appreciate swimming water.

Aylesbury

calm • non-flyer • excellent table bird • moderate layer • needs water to breed

TYPE: **heavy** • WEIGHT: **drake 10–12½ lb (4.5–5.4 kg), duck 9–11 lb (4.1–5 kg)** • COLORS: **white with pink-white bill**

The English town of Aylesbury in Buckinghamshire is synonymous with this big white farm duck. The breed was known during the early eighteenth century and historically Aylesbury ducks were walked from the vale of Aylesbury to London for sale, a distance of about 40 miles (65 km). They stopped along the way at drovers' inns, which had special yards for the ducks. Their feet were covered with tar and sawdust as protection during their walk. Once the railway was built, the birds were put on the trains. J. K. Fowler wrote in 1850 that "in one night, a ton weight of ducklings from six to eight weeks old are taken by rail from Aylesbury and the villages round to the metropolis." The ducks were so valuable to the villagers that they were kept inside the cottages. One such unsanitary area of Aylesbury was known as Duck End. These overcrowded conditions were grim to say the least, for both the "duckers" and their unfortunate charges. New sanitary arrangements in the mid-nineteenth

Aylesbury males – note the flesh-color of the bills.

century saw a decline in production in this way.

In the 1870s, the Pekin duck was brought from China to the UK and crossed with the native Aylesbury, and the original breed was lost. In the 1943 edition of his book *Ducks and Duck Keeping*, Charles Roscoe states that: "Strictly speaking, there are two varieties, the pure utility type and the exhibition type. There is in practice a vast difference between the two." Confusion still abounds, with the Aylesbury ingrained in folk memory and people eagerly calling any large white duck an Aylesbury. The exhibition Aylesbury was immensely popular in Victorian times, where its snowy-white color and impressive size in the show pen drew huge admiration. Sadly, many were seriously overfed and suffered as a result. The exhibition Aylesbury has now become quite rare and in the UK breeders have a "Save the Aylesbury" campaign, while the breed is considered critically rare in the US.

Looks

Both sexes are pure white with blue eyes and bright orange legs. These need to be strong in order to support the large body, which should be long, broad and very deep. A true Aylesbury has a distinctive pink-white or flesh-colored bill: if the bill is orange, the bird is not a purebred Aylesbury but a commercial type with Pekin blood.

Personality

This is a placid breed. It loves to eat, quickly converting its food into weight. An Aylesbury rarely, if ever, flies.

Uses

This is an excellent table bird and a moderate egg layer, producing anything from around 30 to upwards of 100 eggs per year.

Day to day

The Aylesbury needs a varied and nutritious diet but should not be allowed to become obese, especially if it is going to breed. Provide it with enough space to walk around to help control its weight. This large duck needs swimming water in order to mate successfully, and it will then raise its own brood.

Aylesbury female

Cayuga

beautiful plumage • calm • hardy • good forager • dual purpose

TYPE: **heavy** • WEIGHT: **drake 8 lb (3.6 kg), duck 7 lb (3.2 kg)** • COLORS: **black with lustrous green sheen**

There is a traditional story that attributes this breed to a miller living in Duchess County, New York, who is said to have trapped a pair of wild black ducks in 1809 and then left them to settle on his pond and rear their broods. The ducks were then introduced into the Finger Lakes region of New York State in 1840. In 1863 the breed became known as the Cayuga, after a lake in the north of the state which in turn was named after the native Cayuga people. Despite its

The beetle-green sheen covers the whole body, down to the little curly tail.

dark meat, the breed was the principle duck for meat in the US until the introduction of the Pekin in 1873, and was included in the American Poultry Association Standard of Perfection in 1874. The Cayuga was introduced to the UK in the same decade. In 1885, William Cook wrote in *Poultry Breeder and Feeder*: "They fatten quicker than any breed I have kept yet. They are a splendid flavour, though rather dark in flesh. They are often kept as a fancy duck."

Looks

The breed carries itself nearly horizontally and has a large head with a long, wide bill and attractive, bold eyes. This and the graceful neck complement its long, broad body and beautiful plumage, which is black overlaid with a beetle-green sheen. The bill is black, the eyes dark brown, and the legs black.

Personality

This breed is hardy but quiet and calm. If allowed to forage, they are very efficient. Younger birds can

and do fly so you will need to clip their wings.

Uses

This is a good table bird, if you like dark meat. It also lays from 70 to over 100 eggs per year. As with the Black East Indian (see page 106), the first eggs have a sooty layer overlaying the white. In the US they report light gray, blue and green eggs as well.

Day to day

Provide a decent-sized pond to help maintain the plumage in good condition. The Cayuga is a good sitter and will raise her own brood. A breed with a long history, many people today are re-discovering this striking duck breed and finding that the plumage makes it an exciting challenge for exhibition purposes. With it's wild ancestors in mind, it does enjoy having some range so it can live and breed naturally.

Cayuga duck

Muscovy

distinct crest • strong personality • dedicated forager • dual purpose • excellent flyer

TYPE: heavy • WEIGHT: drake 10–14 lb (4.5–6.3 kg), duck 5–7 lb (2.3–3.2 kg) • COLORS: many, including white-winged black, blue, and chocolate; black, white, blue, chocolate whole colors; black-and-white; blue-and-white; chocolate-and-white

Duck Breeds

All domestic ducks derive from the Mallard, except the Muscovy. This is a perching duck and is thought to be related to a tree duck from South America. There is small wild population in Texas and other feral breeding populations elsewhere in North America. This is a highly adaptable bird: there are accounts of Muscovies being domesticated by Native American cultures, and they spread to the UK and the rest of the world with the development of trade routes.

In 1885, famous poultryman and breeder William Cook stated in *Poultry Breeder and Feeder* that: "This breed is rather peculiar in both colour and formation. The drake is very much larger than the duck, weighing almost as heavy again," which is still true today. He speaks of drakes being "spiteful to fowls" and that they "will at times kill chickens." J. B. Merrett, editor of the *New Zealand Poultry Journal* was not a fan of the breed and wrote in 1908 that "they are wild and terrible birds to fly. They are also of a quarrelsome disposition."

Yet Muscovies have always had a keen following of those who don't expect them to behave like usual domestic ducks. A recent comment on the Domestic Waterfowl website was obviously written by someone who knows and loves the breed: "The nicest character of any of the breeds with a pronounced sense of humour, very intelligent and head of any escape committee."

Looks

The Muscovy's carriage is low – the startling factor is the head, with its crest of feathers that raise in alarm. It has caruncles (these are fleshy protruberances) on the face and over the base of the bill, which is wide, strong, and slightly curved.

In terms of color, both sexes are the same. The color should be clear and markings regular and symmetrical. The white-winged varieties come in black, blue, and chocolate and are this color throughout, with white just on the wing coverts. The solid colors of black, white, blue, and chocolate are even throughout, although the black may have a metallic-green sheen. If black-and-white, blue-and-white, or chocolate-and-white, the markings must be regular.

Personality

People are either Muscovy fans and find them full of personality, independent, and charming, or not, and think them ugly and difficult.

Uses

A moderate layer producing 70–100 large white eggs, the Muscovy is also a good table bird.

Day to day

Muscovies need enough water just to be able to splash in or maybe float on briefly. However, they do need to forage and eat grubs and even small mammals, so keep them away from small pets. As they are "tree ducks" they have very sharp claws for perching. Muscovies are excellent flyers and some keepers allow them to do so, as they seem to return home when they are happy with where they live. However, it may be more prudent to clip their wings, at least initially. A Muscovy is a superb mother and is quite capable of raising her own brood. She will sit for up to 35 days rather than the 28 that is normal with other domestic ducks.

Muscovy ducks come in a range of colors.

Pekin

docile • good forager • excellent table bird • good layer • non-flyer

TYPE: **heavy** • WEIGHT: **drake 9 lb (4.1 kg), duck 8 lb (3.6 kg)** • COLOR: **white**

These ducks supposedly date back to 2500 BC in China and are part of the history of the country. They were spotted there in the late nineteenth century by a Mr. McGrath and brought to the US in 1873. They were an almost instant success and soon overtook the native Cayuga as the principle table bird. The breed reached the UK at the same time and was greeted with similar enthusiasm. By 1885, in *Poultry Breeder and Feeder,* William Cook was saying: "This breed is often taken for Aylesbury ducks, because they are white in plumage." He also talked of the yellowish hue on their feathers, something still noticeable today. Cook was enthusiastic about the breed and chronicled his crossings with Rouen, Muscovy, and Cayuga. He also rated them as excellent egg layers.

By 1947 F. J. S. Chatterton had become equally enthusiastic, and wrote rather whimsically in *Ducks and Geese and How to Keep Them* of the way the feathers grow in the drake's head as being "rather pretty" and "giving them a unique appearance." He was more definite about their care, saying that "as pure breeds they do not fatten well in confinement." Today, over 60 years later, we still note that this breed does better if given some range. There can be no doubt that the Pekin has had considerable influence worldwide on the production of birds for the table.

Looks

The carriage of the Pekin is almost upright and the head is large, broad, and round with dark blue eyes. Strong, well-set-back legs support a broad, full body, and a stern carried just above the ground. The plumage does not show as tight but is almost fluffy and very abundant. The Standards describe the plumage as deep cream or cream, but the older books talk about white overlaid with a yellow tinge. The bill is bright orange as opposed to the Aylesbury's classic pink-white.

Personality

The Pekin is amenable and docile. Although large, it likes to forage and range but does not fly.

Uses

This is a quick-maturing, high meat-yielding table bird. In the UK, 70–100 eggs per year is the average, but keepers in the US expect up to 200.

Day to day

These ducks are not suitable to keep as a group in muddy conditions due to the openness of their feathering. They will become very dirty, very quickly. They therefore need clean, dry conditions and water to wash in. They also need space to range. The open plumage does attract mites far more readily than that of other duck breeds, so keep on top of parasite prevention. It is also susceptible to fly strike. Most birds will go broody and hatch eggs, unless they come from a commercial strain.

Pair of Pekin ducks

Rouen

beautiful • calm • good forager • non-flyer • slow maturing

TYPE: **heavy** • WEIGHT: **drake 10–12½ lb (4.5–5.4 kg), duck 9–11 lb (4.1–5 kg)** • COLORS: **Mallard markings**

Duck Breeds

The original name could have been Rouen, Rhone, or Roan, but it is generally acknowledged that this duck was first heard of in the eighteenth century in Normandy, France, around the city of Rouen. By the early 1900s it was prevalent, having been introduced to all countries including the US, where it was admitted to the Standard of Perfection in 1874. It originally reached the US as a general-purpose farm duck, imported by D. W. Lincoln of Massachusetts. By 1885, William Cook in the UK was recommending the Rouen somewhat dubiously in *Poultry Breeder and Feeder*, with the advice that "this breed are brown and do not show the dirt when they have no water to wash themselves in," although he did concede that "the drakes are very handsome."

The Australasian poultry keepers were a little more encouraging – *Utility Poultry Farming*, published in 1908, stated that: "The Rouen Duck is a fine market bird." The authors speculated that some thought the name might have come from the word roan on account of the color,

but rejected this idea as they felt the color was definitely brighter than this. It was the colors and impressive size of the Rouen that made it an obvious choice for keen exhibitors in the early twentieth century and much effort was put into breeding for color. Today it is mainly used for exhibition.

Looks

Sometimes it's hard to believe all domestic ducks except the Muscovy originated from the Mallard, but not when you look at this giant of the duck world. As with the Mallard, the drake has a green head, white collar, claret breast, and a blue patch on the wing,

Rouen females

although the Rouen is even brighter in color and much larger in size than the Mallard. The duck is a rich brown with dark brown feather markings and a blue patch on the wings. The carriage is low to the ground and the bird has a large head and a long, flat, wide bill. The body is sometimes described as box shaped.

Personality
Luckily, this very large bird has a calm, tame temperament. Slow to mature, it takes up to 20 weeks to get adult feathers – compared to seven to eight weeks for commercial breeds. It likes to forage and needs to keep active because despite its bulk, its strong legs are made for walking and inactivity will result in it becoming too fat.

Uses
The Rouen produces very tasty, rather dark meat but is now kept primarily for its beauty as an exhibition bird. Its egg-laying capability varies according to the strain, but around 100 eggs per year can be considered a good performance.

Day to day
The Rouen can manage with a container for a pond and splashing water. Unlike most of the light ducks, this breed does better with a smaller ratio of ducks to drakes – a trio or no more than three ducks is considered best. It is not the easiest of breeders and young ducklings will need protection from the weather even if they are with their mother.

Duck Breeds

Rouen male

Rouen Clair

beautiful • calm • keen forager • good layer • poor flyer

TYPE: heavy • WEIGHT: drake 7½–9 lb (3.4–4.1 kg), duck 6½–7½ lb (2.9–3.4 kg) • COLORS: light Mallard markings

Also known as the Duclair Duck and developed for the farmyard, probably by crossbreeding, the Rouen Clair later became popular for exhibiting and the first Standard for the UK was introduced in 1982. The breed originated in France: in 1880 Miss May Arnold, writing in *The Live Stock Journal*, believed that it was "the remains of an old Norman duck preserved by special circumstances." It is hard to find a reference to the Rouen Clair in duck books from the 1900s to the 1940s, but in his 1947 publication *Ducks and Geese*, F. J. S. Chatterton does mention that in France there are two varieties of Rouen – "the Dark and the Light." He was not a fan of the latter, describing the coloring as "washy" but also admitting that "some of the best specimens are large, shapely birds, nearly approaching that of the Darks." A few years earlier Charles Roscoe had pursued a similar theme in *Runner Ducks* and talked about exhibition-type Rouens, which are possibly the Rouen breed, and utility types, which might bear more resemblance to the Rouen Clair. Whatever the explanation, these ducks shine in the show-pen.

Looks

Like the Rouen, this breed has Mallard coloring but in a lighter version. The bird is smaller and more upright than the Rouen. Its notable feature is that it is quite long from beak to end of tail – ideally 35 in (90 cm).

Personality

Again like the Rouen, this bird has a calm temperament. It, too, likes to forage and is a poor flyer.

Uses

Kept primarily for exhibition, nevertheless at between 100 and 200 eggs per year, the Rouen Clair's egg-laying performance is much better than that of the Rouen, due no doubt to its development as a dual-purpose duck.

Day to day

The Rouen Clair can manage with a container for a pond and splashing water, but a pond is ideal. It needs space to forage so that it does not become overweight. For successful breeding, provision of swimming water is advisable.

Rouen Clair male and females

Rouen male and female

Saxony

very attractive • gentle • quick maturing • active forager • good all-rounder

TYPE: heavy • WEIGHT: drake 8 lb (3.6 kg), duck 7 lb (3.2 kg) • COLORS: combination, including rusty-red, oatmeal, blue-gray, and silver

The Saxony duck was bred in the 1930s by Albert Franz in East Germany, from Rouen, German Pekin, and Blue Pomeranian ducks, to improve on their utility qualities. He wanted to shorten the maturing time of the Rouen and breed in a light underneath to eliminate dark pin feathers on a carcass. It was an initial success, but World War II put an end to that and Franz was left to salvage what he could in 1952 from local stock. The breed proved as popular as it had been 25 years earlier as a table bird and good egg layer, but its beautiful color impressed exhibitors as well, just as it does today. The Saxony reached the US in 1984 and was admitted to the Standard of Perfection in 2000.

Looks

It is difficult to breed the Saxony's markings exactly to show standard, but ideally the drake's head and neck should be blue-gray down to a clearly defined white neck ring about ¼ in (5 mm) wide. Below this, the breast and shoulders are rusty red with slight silver lacing. Underneath the body is oatmeal, while the back and rump are blue-gray. The duck has a deep apricot-buff head and neck with a white eye line above and below the eye. There is no neck ring, which if present would be considered a serious fault. The back is a paler buff and the wing feathering shows gray and oatmeal towards the wing tips. In both sexes the bill is yellow and the legs are orange, overall creating an unusual and attractive combination of colors.

Personality

This bird is gentle and an active forager, so provide plenty of space.

Uses

This quick-maturing breed is ideal for the table but is also a good layer, producing around 150 eggs per year. It's a challenge for breeders to achieve the correct color for exhibition purposes, making this a duck for everyone.

Day to day

The Saxony can be successful in brooding its own young as long as it is not overweight, so be sure to encourage its foraging instincts to ensure it gets plenty of exercise.

Saxony male

Saxony female

Blue Swedish

beautiful plumage • calm • keen forager • good small-farm bird • dual purpose

TYPE: **heavy** • WEIGHT: **drake 8 lb (3.6 kg), duck 7 lb (3.2 kg)** • COLORS: **blue with white bib**

Blue ducks have been noted in poultry writings since Victorian times. In Europe it was believed that this color made the ducks exceptionally hardy and more difficult for predators to see. The Blue Swedish is thought to have been bred in parts of northern Europe that were under Sweden's control in the mid-nineteenth century, hence the name. It reached the US in 1884 and was included in the Standard of Perfection in 1904.

Writing in *Ducks and Geese and How to Keep Them* in 1947, F. J. S. Chatterton remarked that: "All blue breeds of poultry have a tendency to go 'mouse colored' especially if left exposed to the weather."

Blue Swedish female

Looks

The head of this duck is oval in shape and the body large and broad. Nevertheless, it carries itself in a lively manner. The head color of the drake is dark blue with a greenish sheen, while the duck's is simply dark blue. For both sexes, the plumage is a uniform shade of slate-blue, strongly laced with a darker blue shade. They have an upside-down, heart-shaped white bib. Even the bills are blue – dark blue in the drake and slate-blue in the duck – although green is also seen. The legs are orange-black in the drake, blue-brown in the duck.

Personality

Ideal for pastures and orchards, this duck loves to forage and has the calm temperament of a backyard or small-farm duck. It also makes an excellent pet.

Uses

An ideal table bird, the Blue Swedish can also lay around 150 eggs per year. Because of the spectacular color, it is a popular choice for exhibition, and the challenge of producing a truly blue bird is one that breeders relish.

Day to day

This breed does not enjoy close confinement so provide plenty of space for it to range. The duck will go broody and raise her own young.

Group of Blue Swedish ducks

Silver Appleyard

ornamental • calm • active forager • quick maturing • good all-rounder

TYPE: **heavy** • WEIGHT: **drake 8–9 lb (3.6–4.1 kg), duck 7–8 lb (3.2–3.6 kg)** • COLOR: **silver effect**

Reginald Appleyard called his Priory Waterfowl Farm at Ixworth in Suffolk "England's leading Stud of ducks and geese" and his adverts in Victor Birtwhistle's *Duck Keeping*, published in 1946, described 12 breeds of geese, 26 breeds and varieties of ducks, 30 acres of grass, a natural river, streams, and pools. It spoke of wins at all shows, with Silver and Bronze Medals at "National" and "*Daily Mail*" Laying Tests. At the bottom of the adverts it stated: "Originator and Breeder of White Ixworths and White Ixworth Bantams." Yet of his most famous duck, the Silver Appleyard, there is no mention.

This is a bit of a mystery, since Appleyard developed the duck to match the high egg-laying ducks of the day and provide meat for the table, and he largely succeeded. But by the time he died in 1964, well respected throughout the world for his knowledge of poultry, the breed was not yet standardized. It arrived in the US in the 1960s, but it wasn't really until the late 1970s that respected breeder Tom Bartlett stimulated interest in the large version of the Appleyard, working from a picture painted of the original breed in 1947 by the well-known poultry artist E. G. Wippell. Bartlett also developed the Miniature Appleyard. In 1998, the American Poultry Association held a qualifying meet for the inclusion of the Appleyard in the American Standard of Perfection, and officially recognized the Silver Appleyard duck in 2000. Today it is kept more widely and valued in show pens worldwide, although it also still fulfills Mr. Appleyard's original aim of breeding a good layer of white eggs that matures quickly for the table.

Looks

A lively, slightly erect duck, the Silver Appleyard could be described as chunky with its broad, compact, well-rounded body. In the drake, the head and neck are dark green with a silver-flecked throat to a silver-white ring around the neck. Below the ring and on the breast the bird is a claret color and the feathers are fringed with white. Underneath, the body is silver. Like the Mallard, the drake has an iridescent speculum (back part of the wing feathers). The duck is equally ornamental, with a silver-white head and neck, and flecked through from the crown and along the back and rump with brown-gray. Underneath she is a creamy white, again with an iridescent speculum. The legs of both sexes are orange.

Personality

An active forager with a good appetite, this bird puts on weight and matures quickly. It has a calm disposition.

Uses

The Silver Appleyard is a truly ornamental bird with strong utility qualities. It is an excellent layer of 100–180 (or more) large white eggs, a fast-maturing breed for the table, and is also a good exhibition bird.

Day to day

The Silver Appleyard needs space and opportunity to forage, plus a good layer ration in order to produce a high number of eggs. It can be kept as a flock for laying or as a trio for breeding.

Silver Appleyard trio

Light goose breeds

This classification of geese includes the best layers and most active birds. They are also the smallest birds of the three goose sections, and cover a wide range of types from the noisy Chinese to the diminutive crested Roman goose.

Chinese

elegant and upright • noticeable knob on bill • good guard goose • best laying breed

TYPE: **light** • WEIGHT: **gander 10-12½ lb (4.5–5.4 kg), goose 8–10 lb (3.6–4.5 kg)** • COLORS: **brown, gray, white**

Along with the heavy African breed, this goose did not originate from the Greylag as did all of the European breeds, but from the wild Asiatic Swan goose. This ancestry can be seen particularly in the brown variation. The Chinese goose must have been in the UK by the time of the first poultry show in 1845 which included classes for "Knobbed or Asiatic" geese. The breed lost popularity until around the 1930s, when it was recorded by respected poultry breeder Reginald Appleyard – who was primarily interested in utility birds – that the Chinese goose often laid 60 eggs per season, sometimes up to 100. In 1908, *Utility Poultry Farming for Australasia* acknowledged that "the birds are good layers, laying from 50–60 eggs in each year."

In the UK in 1932, *The Feathered World Year Book* contained an article by well-known breeder Miss M. G. Newman which mentioned the two strains we still see, the ornamental bird and the American utility strain. Today, exhibitors prefer the smaller American show strain, no doubt

developed from the utility. The first of these were imported from the US in the 1970s by respected waterfowl collector and breeder Christopher Marler.

Miss Newman talked of the highest egg record known being 140 eggs, but pointed out that the genuine American strain would always expect 70 or 80. She said that "the breed is rapidly spreading to all parts of the country, from Wales to Cornwall, to the Midlands and the North," and concluded:

"For a combination of unusual beauty and profit-earning qualities, the Utility Chinese goose is without a rival."

Looks

This is an elegant goose that stands very erect. The rounded knob on the bill is warm to the touch and in some countries can be in danger of damage from frostbite. The brown or gray goose has a dark stripe extending from the crown of the head all the way down the back

White Chinese goose

Brown-gray Chinese

of the neck. The underside of the neck, the breast and the underbody are light fawn with cream around the throat. The body and thighs are a rich brown to fawny gray, and the underbody is white towards the stern. In mature birds, the black bill and knob are separated from the head by a narrow band of creamy white feathers. The feet are orange. The white bird is pure white with blue eyes and orange-yellow legs. The bill and knob are orange.

Personality

These geese are often described as chatty – but the neighbors might call them noisy! Because they are so talkative, they make excellent guard geese and are often kept for that purpose. In addition, they are graceful and refined. As with any geese, they can be protective and defensive if scared and in some circumstances – say, children behaving inappropriately – might give a painful nip with their strong bill.

Uses

This is a very economical breed, producing up to 100 eggs per year that can be sold or incubated, as well as dark but lean, non-greasy meat. In the late nineteenth century they were used in the US as "weeder" geese but, like all breeds, if there is a choice they are more likely to select grass as their favorite food. They also cannot distinguish vegetables from weeds!

Day to day

The Chinese goose is not known for flying, so is happy around the holding as long as it has lots to do and see, and plentiful grazing. As the feet are in proportion to the bird's size, they are not as likely to paddle the ground as other breeds.

Pilgrim

docile • good forager • hardy • good table bird • auto-sexing

TYPE: light • weight: gander 14–18 lb (6.3–8.2 kg), goose 12½–16 lb (5.4–7.3 kg) • COLORS: white gander, gray goose

Some have theorized that the ancestors of this breed were taken to the New World with the Pilgrims in 1620. It is thought that this type of goose was widely seen on farms and smallholdings in the UK by the late nineteenth century but it was not classified – they were just considered common geese. What *is* known is that the breed was first standardized in the US in the 1930s as a result of work by Oscar Grow

in the Midwest. He named them Pilgrims in homage to his family's "pilgrimage" from Missouri as a result of the Depression, although this does not preclude a connection with the Pilgrims' original geese. In the UK, a few exhibitors took up the breed and it gained credibility, although it is still relatively low in numbers. Today, it is considered a rare breed in the US.

Looks

As it can be hard to tell the difference between sexes in some goose breeds, these are welcome for the very clear difference: a snow-white gander and a softly gray goose. She may have white near her bill and characteristic white "spectacles," and the white markings will increase as she grows older. Both sexes have orange legs, but the gander has blue eyes and the goose hazel-brown. They have full, plump bodies and tight plumage.

Personality

The Pilgrim has a quiet and docile disposition. It is hardy and an industrious forager.

Uses

This medium-sized goose is primarily a good table bird.

Day to day

Because it is easy to distinguish the sexes, you can be sure you have the correct ratio of males to females (one gander to up to five geese). Take care you are not sold a "Pilgrim" that is in fact simply a small white gander from one of the other white breeds. If this happens, the resulting stock will not carry the auto-sexing genes for the distinguishing coloring. Pilgrims generally make good parents, although in some parts of the US fertility problems are reported, perhaps due to inbreeding.

Female with characteristic face markings

Pilgrim female

Roman (Roman Tufted)

compact • active • kind – good all-rounder • easy breeder

TYPE: **light** • WEIGHT: **gander 12½–14 lb (5.4–6.3 kg), goose 10–12½ lb (4.5–5.4 kg)** • COLOR: **white**

A lively Roman goose.

This classical breed has its origins in Ancient Rome – the geese herded across the Alps in that period were most likely early examples. The Roman goose reached the UK early in the twentieth century where it became a small table goose.

In the *Feathered World Year Book* of 1932, Stanley Street-Porter said of the breed: "I have bred them for many years and am of the opinion that they are the best and most profitable geese for utility purposes in existence." He summed up: "I have found them prolific as breeders, easy to rear, quick growers, good feeders and good sellers." A flock of these diminutive, sparkling white, busy geese grazing on green summer grass is a compelling sight.

In the US this breed is usually crested and is known as the Roman Tufted.

Looks

This is an active goose with a horizontal carriage, short to medium-length neck and a compact, deep, broad body. It is white all over with orange-pink legs and bill and light blue eyes. In the crested version, there is a tuft of feathers on the crown of the head that is far more discreet than in crested ducks. In the US, the Standard requires a crest. Make sure you are buying Roman geese rather than undersized or young birds from a larger white or commercial breed.

Personality

Romans are robust birds. They are active and lively, but usually have a charming temperament.

Uses

This breed is kept for exhibition and as a small but meaty table goose. It is also a good layer, producing 30–60 eggs per year.

Day to day

Romans are good breeders, and one gander should be able to breed with up to five geese. If you want a smaller goose with a friendly temperament then this may well be the choice for you. It's only fault for goose keepers historically was its small stature which meant that it could not mature to great weights, but for today's smaller families and keeping for exhibition and pleasure, it is a perfect choice.

Roman goose

Sebastopol

ornamental • frizzled feathers • dual purpose • non-flyer

TYPE: light • WEIGHT: gander 12½–16 lb (5.4–7.3 kg), goose 10–14lb (4.5–6.3 kg) • COLORS: white, buff

This goose originated in Central Europe and in the 1850s it was known that the birds were widely distributed around the Black Sea and in the Balkans. It arrived in the UK in 1859 and was recognized in the US in 1938, where the special curly feathers were much sought after for use in feather products. In the 1966 *British Waterfowl Association Yearbook*, Mrs. Francis Michael of Crawley advertised "Ornamental Domestic Geese: Sebastapol – Original Curly and Sebastapol – Appleyard's Long Feathered," so clearly Reginald Appleyard must have become interested in what many people called, not unkindly, the "pantomime goose." In the same yearbook another breeder, Lieutenant-Colonel A. A. Johnson, was listed as a seller of exhibition and utility stock for the breed. Today, the Sebastopol is popular in the show pen, although really correct exhibition specimens are difficult to breed.

Looks

There are two types: the Frizzle, and the Smooth-breasted or Trailing Frizzle. Both are recognized. In the Frizzle, only the feathers of the head and upper neck are smooth. All the feathers on the rest of the bird are curled. This is achieved by the flexible spine of the feather itself – the lack of strong spines means the bird cannot fly. In good examples, the curls should spiral and the back and wing feathers will almost touch the ground. In the Smooth-breasted, the head, neck, breast, belly, and paunch are smooth-feathered, while on the back the long feathers curl and spiral down, sometimes to the ground. In this type, the legs and feet should not be visible. Both types come in two colors, white and buff (which is even-colored). The eyes are bright blue in the white and brown in the buff, and the legs are orange in both.

Personality

If well handled, these geese become tame and good natured. Some people believe that they are partly descended from the Russian Fighting Goose and can consequently be quite feisty.

Uses

As well as its fairytale looks, this is a good practical breed that lays up to 35 eggs per year and is a good table bird.

Day to day

Because the plumage is loose and either touches or almost touches the ground, the birds should be kept in clean, dry conditions. They still graze grass, but this needs to be an unbroken sward rather than muddy, and they need sufficient water to keep their magnificent plumage clean. If they become dirty it is impossible for them to get all the dirt out of their spiral feathers. Watch out, too, for the gander having muddy feet when he treads the goose. Nevertheless, Sebastopols make good parents and will raise their own broods.

White Sebastapol

Steinbacher

calm • confident • robust • good table bird • poor layer

TYPE: light • WEIGHT: gander 13–15 lb (6–7 kg), goose 11–13 lb (5–6 kg) • COLORS: blue in UK and US; gray, buff elsewhere

Goose Breeds

Geese were specially selected and bred in Eastern Europe and Russia for fighting up until the early twentieth century, when the sport was banned. They were even mentioned in the Russian novel *The Master and Margarita*, published in the 1930s, when Nikanor Ivanovitch says "Ah if it wasn't for my geese!… I've got fighting geese in Lianozovo my dear fellow… they'll die without me, I'm afraid. A fighting bird's delicate, it needs care… Ah, if it wasn't for my geese!"

The Steinbacher was bred as a fighting goose in an unusual cross between a European farm type (descended from the Greylag) and an Asiatic goose (a knobbed goose descended from the Asiatic Swan goose). It was first classified in 1932 as gray and in 1951 the blue color was recognized. It came to the UK via Thuringer in Germany in the 1980s. In the US it is classed as a rare breed and in 2007, Mrs. Krebs and her sons successfully showed a Steinbacher to take the Best Rare Fowl at the Ohio National show where nearly 4,400 birds where shown.

Looks

This is a spectacular blue goose with white lacing on the shoulder and wing feathers. It stands proud and erect, as its ancestry would suggest, and is slightly stocky. It has strong legs that are bright orange, as is its bill. The eyes have a narrow yellow ring around them.

Personality

Although they were originally bred as fighting geese, keepers report that these birds have a calm temperament.

Uses

Opinions vary as to the Steinbacher's laying ability, but it is not generally regarded as of any particular note. It does, however, make a good table bird and a lovely pet.

Day to day

Although good with humans, this breed can be sharp with other geese, especially gander-on-gander during the breeding season. The goose can be an erratic broody.

Steinbacher goose

Group of Steinbacher geese

Medium goose breeds

As the description implies, these are the breeds that fall between the really heavy, meaty breeds and the lighter ones that tend to be better layers. Some of the best hardy table birds come into this category, including two breeds that, unusually, were developed in the UK from original farmyard geese.

Brecon Buff

exceptionally hardy • alert and active • docile • good table bird • rarely flies

TYPE: medium • WEIGHT: gander 16–20 lb (7.3–9.1 kg), goose 14–18 lb (6.3–8.2 kg) • COLOR: buff

Goose Breeds

This breed was developed in the 1930s from a buff "sport" of traditional geese from hill farms in Brecon, Wales, by Rhys Llewellyn of Swansea. The aim was a truly hardy goose that would provide a smaller table bird with minimum human intervention. To this end, Llewellyn kept his geese in quite harsh conditions and was pleased with how well they did, ranging freely on a large grass area. Today, exhibitors enjoy the challenge of breeding these birds to the standard, buff being a difficult color to achieve.

Looks

These birds should be a deep and even shade of buff, with the goose usually darker than the gander. The eyes are dark brown and the legs pink – they must not be orange. Check this to ensure you have purchased genuine Brecon Buffs. From the breed's harsh origins the geese developed genetics which ensured a good, tight plumage.

Personality

This is an active, alert goose. It has a docile temperament and can become very tame. It rarely flies.

Uses

The Brecon Buff is a compact table bird, ideal for small farms.

Day to day

Bred to live hardily, this goose readily converts food to meat – because it was developed to range large areas, you will need sufficient space and grazing for it to realize its full potential. The Brecon Buff will brood its own goslings.

Below Resting Brecon Buff

Right Brecon Buff goose

Buff Back

very eye-catching • calm and friendly • rarely flies • good all-rounder

TYPE: **medium** • WEIGHT: **gander 18–22 lb (8.2–10 kg), goose 16–20 lb (7.3–9.1 kg)**
• COLOR: **saddleback buff**

Goose Breeds

Pied geese have been known for many years and are associated with the Baltic. In 1966, Mrs. M. A. R. Hunt wrote an enthusiastic article in the *British Waterfowl Association Yearbook* extolling the virtues of the Buff Back, but bemoaning that "their origin is still shrouded in mists." She also stated her opinion that: "This breed is not well known and I think that it should be." She credited the Buff Back with good looks and intelligence and recommended keeping them as pets, guard geese, and for their table and egg-laying qualities. Mrs. Hunt ended her article by saying: "In fact this is one domestic breed which I have been quite unable to fault." The situation hasn't changed since.

Looks

The markings on this goose are very regular. The head is a solid buff color, there is a heart shape of buff on the back and also buff on the thighs, all on a white base. The eyes are blue and the bill and legs orange. The bird has a horizontal carriage with quite long wings and the body is plump and meaty. The legs are sturdy.

The Grey Back shares the origins of the Buff Back and is very similar in shape and markings, this time in grey. Don't confuse it with the Pomeranian (see page 178), which is easy to do. The difference is that the Grey Back (and the Buff) is dual-lobed in the paunch – the part of the underside that runs from just in front to just behind its legs.

Personality

This goose has a calm and friendly disposition. It rarely flies.

Uses

This is a good all-round goose producing a fair-sized carcass. It is also a reasonable egg layer, producing 20–30 eggs per year. Its supporters say it makes a charming family pet.

Day to day

Developed from farm birds in Europe, this goose is used to domestication but likes space to graze. It is a good broody.

Buff Back group

Pair of Buff Back geese

Pomeranian

hardy • strong personality • excellent grazer • good guard goose • dual purpose

TYPE: medium • WEIGHT: gander 18–24 lb (8.2–10.9 kg), goose 16–20 lb (7.3–9.1 kg) • COLORS: saddleback buff; gray, white whole colors

Easily confused with the Buff and Grey Backs (see page 176), this breed originated in the challenging weather conditions on farms in northern Germany and has earned its reputation for hardiness as a result. The geese contributed hugely to the income of these farms with their meat, "goose dripping," and feathers.

Pomeranian goose

Looks

When pied, this white goose is boldly marked with a dark gray head and a heart-shaped saddle on its back. There are patches of gray on the thighs. The bill is reddish or orange-pink, the legs orange-red and the eyes blue. It also comes in whole colors: gray with brown eyes and white with blue eyes. In regards to shape, the crown of the head tends to be flat with the head broad and the neck quite thick towards a body that is plump, deep, and meaty.

The Pomeranian is a distinct breed and is distinguished from the Buff and Grey Backs by having a single lobe in the paunch – the part of the underside that runs from just in front to just behind its legs – which is double in other pied breeds. In the US, the other saddlebacks are usually included with this breed.

Personality

This breed is intelligent and often has a strong personality. A very alert watcher, it is less noisy than the Chinese. Some ganders can be quite dominant towards both people and other geese. Due to low numbers, the Pomeranian can suffer from inbreeding in some strains.

Uses

Developed to be an all-round farm goose, it is very meaty and lays a reasonable number of eggs – depending on the strain, up to 40 or 50 per year. It is also an exceptionally good guard goose.

Day to day

Pomeranian geese are excellent grazers. They also make very good parents.

Pair of Pomeranians

West of England

calm and friendly • hardy • keen forager • good table bird • auto-sexing

TYPE: medium • WEIGHT: gander 16–20 lb (7.3–9.1 kg), goose 14–18 lb (6.3–8.2 kg) • COLORS: white gander, saddleback gray goose

Goose Breeds

Like the Pilgrim, the origins of this breed are thought to lie in the British farmyard goose of a couple of centuries ago. It gets its name from the area in which it was kept, in the county of Devon. It was standardized in the UK in 1999. Interestingly, a photograph of an alert flock in the 1966–1967 *British Waterfowl Association Yearbook* is captioned "West of England Pilgrims at Furzey Park."

Looks
The gander is pure white, while the goose has a gray-and-white head and neck, a gray saddle marking across her back and gray patches on her thighs. The bill in both sexes is orange, as are the legs, and the eyes are blue.

Personality
Originating from farm stock, these birds offer all the attributes of farm geese: they are hardy, good foragers and grazers, and have a pleasant temperament.

Uses
A reasonable layer, producing 20–30 eggs per year, this is also a good table and exhibition goose.

Day to day
The fact that you can tell the sexes apart easily is very useful when buying. Take care that you are purchasing genuine stock, as it is relatively easy for unscrupulous sellers to pass off other medium-sized white ganders as this breed. The breed has not long had a Standard and numbers are relatively low, so for good quality stock you will need to track down a reputable breeder. The birds enjoy grazing on a decent-sized range.

A resting female

West of England female

Heavy goose breeds

This section includes the largest and arguably most impressive breeds of goose. From the stately African to the colorful American Buff, the world-famous Embden to the placid Toulouse, all these geese are well known and widely appreciated.

African

massive • confident and gentle • noisy • moderate layer • long lived

TYPE: **heavy** • WEIGHT: gander 22–28 lb (10–12.7 kg), goose 18–24 lb (8.2–10.9 kg) • COLORS: **brown, gray, buff, white**

Goose Breeds

Unlike the northern European geese, this breed (like the small Chinese goose) is a descendent of the Asiatic Swan goose, but it is considerably larger than the Chinese breed. As with so many waterfowl, it arrived in the US and UK as a result of the huge increase in world trade the nineteenth century. The brown African was admitted to the American Poultry Association's Standard of Perfection in 1879. The Americans were very enthusiastic about the breed but in the UK it appears to have been less popular, although in 1845 the first poultry show had classes for Asiatic or Knob geese. By the early twentieth century, in New Zealand J. B. Merrett was writing of the Grey African that "they grow the heaviest in the shortest space of time" and praising their laying ability of 40–50 eggs per year, although today's birds do not generally reach this level.

In the 1980s, more stock was imported to the UK from the US and the breed finally became valued once more. In Australia, the Rare Breeds Trust says that the bird is not as heavy as in other countries, and dedicated breeders are working to improve the quality of the geese and increase their numbers. In northern Europe and the US, the African is seen in the show pen and is kept for its impressive size and gentle outlook on life.

Looks

The African is very large with an upright carriage for such a heavy bird – it can stand as much as 3 ft (1 m) high. The head is big and broad, with a large knob protruding from the front of the skull – usually larger in ganders

African male goose

than geese. The lower jaw and top of the neck carry a large dewlap. The body, too, is huge and also long (and almost as wide). It has tight plumage, giving a sleek appearance – that on the neck is likened to velvet.

The brown and gray resemble the colors of the Asiatic Swan goose, with the distinctive brown stripe from the crown of the head down the back of the neck contrasting with the fawn-brown of the body with its shaded feathers. The breast and neck are light fawn. The bill and knob are black and the legs dark orange. The buff is marked in a similar way but is lighter than the brown or gray. It has a pinkish-brown bill and knob. The white is a pure white with a bright orange bill and knob. This color has blue eyes.

Personality

This is a calm and gentle bird. Like the Chinese, it is talkative but nowhere near as loud as its smaller relation.

Uses

The African is a reasonable layer, producing up to 30 eggs per year. It makes a large table bird, but today is kept more for its substantial beauty and to preserve a rare breed. It also makes an impressive exhibition bird.

Pair of African females

Day to day

These geese like to forage and need some space. Due to their size, they require more feeding than most other breeds but should not be allowed to get too fat, so space to move and water to play in will help keep them fit. Mating on water is really helpful, so a pond is a good investment if you plan to keep this breed long term. These are heavy birds with large feet, so well-drained soil and control of the stocking rate are essential. The goose likes to brood but may well flatten her goslings, so the eggs are probably best moved into an incubator.

American Buff

very large • colorful • calm • hardy • good all-rounder

TYPE: **heavy** • WEIGHT: **gander 22–28 lb (10–12.7 kg), goose 20–26 lb (9.1–11.8 kg)** • COLOR: **buff**

This breed was developed in the US – probably from the Pomeranian goose (see page 178), although the American Buff is not saddlebacked. It was developed as a heavy breed solely for its commercial application as an efficient meat producer and was admitted to the American Standard of Perfection in 1947, and its exhibition career began. In the US the breed is classified as medium weight. American Buffs were imported into the UK in the 1970s and 1980s and became popular birds for the show pen.

Looks
This is an upright bird with a medium-long, strong neck, chunky body, and broad tail. Ideally, the color should be buff with no shades of gray and even throughout. The bill and legs are orange and the eyes brown. The American Buff can be confused with the Brecon Buff (see page 174), but it should be much larger. A tufted version can be found in Holland.

Personality
This calm and hardy breed makes a colorful flock against the plentiful green grass on which it likes to graze.

Uses
Developed as a meat breed, the American Buff is a moderate layer of between 10 and 20 eggs per year. It is also favored as an exhibition bird.

Day to day
This large bird requires considerable food to furnish its bulky frame, so plenty of good grass is essential. It also needs lots of splashing water and enjoys swimming if possible. It is also a good natural parent.

American Buff group

American Buff goose

Embden

tallest white goose • active and bossy • good all-rounder • protective of young

TYPE: **heavy** • WEIGHT: **gander 28–34 lb (12.7–15.4 kg), goose 24–28 lb (10.9–12.7 kg)** • COLOR: **white**

Goose Breeds

This breed originated in Germany and is also known as the Emden, which is the twentieth-century spelling of the German port. It was called the Bremans when it first reached the US in the 1820s, having already found favor in the UK. The Victorians took delight in getting these birds as large as possible for exhibition purposes. In the early twentieth century J. B. Merrett, editor of the *New Zealand Poultry Journal*, wrote that these were considered "very practical birds for farmers and pay well for their keeping," with weights quoted

Embden goose stretching its wings.

at 20 lb (9 kg) for ganders and 18 lb (8 kg) for geese. In the 1933 *Feathered World Yearbook*, R. Durrant-Ives advised that: "In picking out exhibition Embdens you want birds with good depth of chest and a round, full chest." Seven Embdens were exhibited at the Crystal Palace show that year.

Looks

This is the archetypal large white farmyard goose. It carries itself confidently and has an elegant neck for its size, an orange bill, and light blue eyes. Many breeders report that the Embden can be sexed at a very early age, as the young males show as a lighter gray than the darker females.

Personality

Embdens can be protective and bossy. They are also very large and are unfazed if young children or household pets such as a small dog or over-curious cat invade their space, but this can result in damage to the weaker party. Take special care to keep them separate from smaller birds, other animals or, indeed, small children.

Uses

The Embden is a moderate layer, producing 20–25 eggs per year. In North America, Embdens are widely raised as table birds since they are hardy and grow well. They are also good for exhibition.

Day to day

Although large, Embdens like to be active so need plenty of space and some water. They do like to sit and breed, but because of their size can easily damage eggs or goslings. In addition, the male becomes very protective, so an incubator would be a safer option. The biggest problem is finding genuine birds – not every large white goose is an Embden! Finding good, purebred examples means searching out a reputable breeder.

Pair of Embdens

Toulouse

very large • tranquil • requires careful management • utility and exhibition types

TYPE: **heavy** • WEIGHT: **gander 26–30 lb (11.8–13.6 kg), goose 20–24 lb (9.1–10.9 kg)** • COLORS: **gray, buff, white**

Goose Breeds

This is a French breed, developed in the south of the country for the table and, in particular, for the production of *pâté de foie gras*. It was imported into the UK in the 1840s and the US a decade later. In 1885, famous poultryman and breeder William Cook described the Toulouse as "a splendid breed. They usually went by the name of 'Grey Geese' with most farmers. They are very upright in appearance, the lower part almost touching the ground." They are also mentioned as a slow-maturing Christmas goose by J. B. Merrett, writing in New Zealand in 1908. In the US, there are two types of Toulouse: the production and the exhibition dewlap. In the UK, there are the utility and the exhibition, but in reality something described as a utility may simply be a gray crossbred, so check out the strain before you buy.

Looks

The Toulouse carries itself in a horizontal manner, at a stately pace. The head is very large and there is a well-developed dewlap (which should be particularly large in exhibition birds) at the top of a long, thick neck. The body is long and broad and the legs short. Something to remember is that the plumage is full and soft, so it is not particularly waterproof and this goose should have shelter. The gray color features feathers edged with white and the goose is white underneath. In the buff, the markings are the same but the gray is replaced with buff. The white is pure white all over with blue eyes, while the other colors have brown eyes. All three have orange legs.

Personality

Large and gentle, this goose is moderately active up to two years old and then becomes tranquil and slow moving. The birds should therefore not be worried by more active geese, nor harassed or frightened. They are quite shy when young and time spent handling and talking to them will result in calmer, more confident adults.

Uses

This goose is a reasonable layer, producing around 30–40 eggs per year. The large exhibition type is really too fat to make a good table bird, so for this purpose choose a utility type.

Day to day

These large geese need access to green food, sufficient water for them to be able to preen, and preferably something that they can at least float in. They do not require large areas as they are not particularly active, but the land needs to be well drained if it is not to be churned up by their large feet. Toulouse make quite good mothers but they are clumsy and may break eggs or tread on goslings. The birds' feathering is soft and open, which means they can be targeted by insects (in hot, humid weather watch out for fly strike, especially if water is limited). For the same reason, they should be kept dry and provided with good shelter. Although easy to work with, they do require more careful management than the hardier breeds.

Toulouse male and female

Wildfowl and Commercial

Wildfowl are still found in the wild and are kept for their beauty and interest, although some breeds are kept in captivity in collections. They have to be kept differently and its best to start with domestics before progressing to these. There are also commercial breeds that have been developed from domestic breeds for characteristics such as quicker maturing, more meat, or better breeding.

Ornamental and wildfowl

All the domestic ducks and geese we have looked at in this book are beautiful, but they are not classified as ornamental. The definition of "ornamental" is a species that is kept for looks alone, and not for another purpose, be it for eggs, meat, or feathers.

From domestic to wild

As well as ducks and geese, ornamentals also include swans. Sometimes ornamentals are referred to as wildfowl, although this term can also mean wild migratory birds. All these waterfowl must usually be kept on a lake or large natural pond, although occasionally they will manage on an artificial pond or in a very large aviary.

It's best to start by keeping domestic waterfowl before moving on to wildfowl – by definition, they are tamer and easier to manage. When you feel that you have gained good experience with this type of bird, you might then want to look at beginning a wildfowl or ornamental collection.

Management

There are two main things to remember in keeping wildfowl:
- Species do not always mix and you will need to learn about different breeds, where they originate from and which birds will co-exist – for example, swans and geese can be an explosive mixture.
- The term "wildfowl" means that even if bred in captivity, these birds can and do fly. You therefore have a choice: to go for pinioned birds (in which the tip of the wing has been removed permanently at one day old), which means they will never be able to fly, or to keep your birds within an aviary-type enclosure, as they will fly over an ordinary fence.

In theory, there is also the option of clipping the flight feathers, but this needs to be done at least once a year and it may be difficult – and traumatic for the birds – to catch them again.

There are advantages to both methods: the pinioned bird can range over a wider area, while an aviary will allow for limited flight. You should also bear in mind

Above Tufted male – these require diving water.

that in many countries there are laws making it illegal to release non-native breeds into the wild, even accidentally, so there may be a legal obligation upon you to keep your ornamentals within the boundaries of your property.

Designing an aviary

There are many attractive ways of designing your aviary, but before you begin you will need to understand the requirements of your ornamentals.

Ducks

Many breeds nest and behave differently to domestic ducks, although having already kept domestic birds you will find many similarities as well.

Perching ducks need to perch and nest in trees. (The only domestic perching duck is the Muscovy – see pages 146–147, but this bird is able to adapt to domestic circumstances as well.) The very beautiful Mandarin duck falls into this category. Perching ducks often rear their ducklings in holes in trees and will therefore need a nestbox. The young ducklings have to get from this to the ground – fortunately, their light weight usually prevents injury, but in the wild it's the predators that might be waiting below that are the problem.

The attractive and lively Tufted duck is one member of a category that needs to be able to dive in order to obtain food. These ducks can be under the water for what may seem a long time but is actually about 30 seconds, and may emerge some distance from where they entered. The dive is usually about 8 ft (2.5 m), which indicates the depth of water such ducks would enjoy. In captivity you would need to provide at least 3 feet (1 meter) depth.

The Mallard is a "dabbler," as are the Teal and the aptly named Shovelers. These birds feed on or near the surface. They love plants, insects, and insect larvae, and are often seen dabbling along the river's edge. Sometimes they do

up-end and you can see their tails sticking out above the water.

When designing an aviary, you can now see that for perching ducks you will need trees, perching places, and higher nestboxes; for divers, some depth of water; and for dabblers, water depth and sustainable feedstuffs around the surface. The enclosure will be the complete home for the birds, so must provide interest for them, shelter, and shade from heat. They will also need protection from wind or severe chill as they are confined and cannot seek out a less exposed place. You can do this by planting tall grasses, reeds, shrubs, and trees, and perhaps also include solid hurdles for added shelter.

Geese

It is just as important to understand how ornamental geese would behave in the wild. You must avoid overstocking: the general rule is no more than ten pairs per 1 acre (0.4 ha), less if the grazing is poor quality or waterlogged. You will also need to reduce the density if you are hoping to breed, because the goslings will need sufficient grazing as well.

Geese require water for swimming as nearly all court and mate on water. Depending on the size of the geese, a pond should be a minimum of 20 in (50 cm) deep and sufficiently large to accommodate the number of birds comfortably. Always start with fewer birds than you think the area will support and go from there. As with domestic geese, ornamentals pair bond and both take a role in rearing the goslings – the goose does the brooding, but the gander protects her and is also actively involved in caring for the young birds.

Protection against predators

As with all waterfowl, protection against a range of predators – the most obvious being foxes – is essential. If you have chosen to pinion your birds, they will not be able to get away and are, in every sense sitting ducks. You will need to protect them by erecting electric

Above Mandarins are strikingly handsome but can fly very well (and do so!).

fencing around the area, shutting the birds inside at night (easier said than done with wildfowl), or by having a night-time aviary to which they return at the end of the day.

In practice, the fencing option is expensive initially but safer, less work in the long run, and less intrusive for you and the birds. A fox-proof fence will need to be at least 6 ft (2 m) high, with a 18-in (45-cm) overhang at the top. It should be sunk into the ground so that a fox cannot dig underneath it. A single-strand electrified wire just above the ground and again along the top of the fence will further reinforce your "keep out" message.

Other predators include domestic pets such as dogs and cats. A cat won't take an adult bird but a dog may. Winged threats such as hawks can take small birds as well as young. Smaller animals such as mink, opossum, stoats, and weasels are a real problem to keep out, although electric fencing will help.

Feeding

Feeding ornamentals is relatively straightforward. You can buy specialist wildfowl pellets to mix with wheat and feed to your birds. As with domestic waterfowl, it's important that all the birds get fed, so you will need an adequate number of feeders – once again, autofeeders will reduce waste. Watch out for surplus food: if there is a lot of waste, either you are feeding too much or for some reason the birds are not eating as much as they should. Whatever the cause, the wasted food will attract vermin such as rats, which are bad for your environment and very hazardous for the birds, especially those that are breeding. You will need to feed extra rations in cold weather and at molting time.

As with domestic waterfowl, the gizzard does the grinding work in the digestive system and it needs grit, so provide the birds with access to this at all times. (See also Feeding, pages 50–53.)

Breeding

If you want to be successful in breeding your own ornamentals, you will need to know your breed. Before you can provide what a pair needs in order to produce young, you need to understand their requirements, including everything from correct positioning and type of nest to the month of brooding. Mandarins, for example, prefer a branch that overhangs the water, while geese tend to choose their own nesting sites and it's then very much up to you to keep them safe from predators, including those that might take the eggs or young. As with domestic ducks, you can also try incubation and broody hens (see pages 74–81).

If you have planned everything properly, a collection of ornamental waterfowl will give you a great deal of pleasure in return for limited work. It will also generate an interest in these beautiful birds that may even take you around the world to see them in their natural environment.

Ornamental checklist

✔ Do your homework on the needs of various breeds and types.

✔ Visit as many waterfowl collections as you can and ask questions. Note such things as which birds are kept together, the layout of the enclosures, the fencing, and so on.

✔ Start small. Begin with a few pairs of birds that are known to live well together and only expand when you know you can cope.

✔ Stick to native breeds to begin with, as they won't require extra heat, different conditions, or specialist feed.

✔ Don't include saltwater ducks such as Eiders until you have gained considerable experience.

✔ Don't overstock: less is definitely more in a successful wildfowl collection.

✔ If you are considering keeping swans, find out all about them and be very careful in mixing them with other species.

✔ Spend time and money planning and constructing your wildfowl enclosure, for the birds' welfare and protection against predators. Remember that it should also look attractive to you!

Wildfowl and Commercial

Commercial breeds

As tastes have changed and demand for increased quantities of food has led to intensive agriculture, so ducks and geese breeds have been developed to cope with the demands made by the modern world.

Characteristics

It's worth remembering – particularly when reading through the duck and goose breed profiles in this book – that nearly all the breeds were purposely evolved to fill a human need at a particular time in history and to fit in with circumstances that were sometimes unique to an area.

One hundred years ago, breeds that we now consider only partly useful and most people keep largely as pets or for their looks, were considered commercial. For example, in the 1930s the charming little Roman goose (see page 166) was valued for its ability to fatten to a small but meaty carcass on grass and feed that included locally available grain and potatoes, while the Silver Appleyard (see page 158), a duck we now value highly for its plumage, was always intended to be a top laying duck.

Of course, the domestic breeds retain their original utility characteristics, but now when we talk about commercial birds we mean the hybrid strains that have been utilized for desirable characteristics and to increase production. Hybrid table ducks have their origins in the early meat-producing breeds, the Aylesbury and Pekin plus the Muscovy (see pages 142, 146, and 148); the egg-producing strains hark back to the original egg duck, the white Indian Runner, and the prolific-laying Khaki Campbell (see pages 128 and 120).

Intensive versus extensive

The duck has become more of an intensive bird than the goose because it will still produce in confined conditions. The goose has steadfastly refused to respond to too much commercialization, still demanding to be kept in a quasi-traditional way with grazing and moderate stocking rates. Intensive farming of any livestock cannot take place if the livestock in question refuses to thrive, and geese have very specific needs. They simply cannot be coerced into laying more or going without grass!

Above Commercial goose breeds do make good pets as well as table birds.

Keeping commercials

For the small flock duck or goose breeder, commercial strains of ducks or geese are fine as long as you know that they are not the purebred equivalent. For example, a large white duck is not a purebred Aylesbury unless it conforms to the Standard laid down by each country's appropriate society. Similarly, a white goose is not necessarily an Embden.

You also need to be aware that commercial table ducks put on a lot of weight in a short time, exactly as they have been designed to do. Many can be on the table within two months of being an egg. Sometimes they can become over-heavy for their legs, although sensible feeding and access to space for exercise will normally solve the problem. For egg-laying strains, the main consideration for high egg-laying hens applies – they will need a good quality ration for their body to be able to cope with the demands made upon it.

Commercial breeds of geese make excellent pets or table birds. It might be possible to buy some older birds from the breeding flock that, although too old for commercial breeding, have many good years left in a private home.

Going commercial

If you decide to take up duck or goose rearing on a commercial basis, make absolutely sure you have a market for the produce. With table ducks and geese, you will need a humane method of slaughter that complies with legal requirements and you will also need to consider plucking. This is very hard work and it is usually quite difficult to find anyone to undertake the task, although there are various plucking machines on the market in two types: wet and dry.

As with any enterprise, it is best to find out as much as you can about it in advance, join the relevant producers organization and start in a small way. These days, duck production too is looking more to free-range and perhaps this will cause more commercial breeds to be developed.

Commercial geese

In one model commercial premises the goose flock are kept in large, free-range pastures with a big, roomy barn for night-time and for laying. The breeding flock is mixed sex with approximately one gander to six females. They are reared together and stay together for the six years they are in the flock. They average 64 eggs with a laying season that begins in late winter and lasts until the late spring/ early summer, and from those eggs an average of 42 goslings are reared. The table geese are reared on pasture and wheat, and are shut in safely at night in a huge shed with a wire front. The way the geese are kept is very much goose led: if they don't get the conditions they need then they don't thrive, breed well or put on weight for the table.

Some established commercial breeds

Legarth Fast-growing white goose with good egg-laying performance and fertility.

Cherry Valley Pekin-type heavyweight meat-producing duck.

Kortlang Development of the Khaki Campbell to produce a super high-laying strain with up to 350 eggs per year.

There are many others, often given the names of the areas where they were developed, such as the Somerset goose. As throughout history, breeders are constantly experimenting with crosses to produce bigger, better, faster-growing, higher egg-laying strains and then naming them.

Wildfowl and Commercial

Questions and Answers

Don't be put off getting ducks or geese because you're not sure about some aspect of their care or welfare. Look through these quick questions for an answer, and then read the relevant in-depth information provided elsewhere in the book.

I'd like to keep ducks for egg laying but I don't want to collect fertile eggs. Is it necessary to have a male in order for the ducks to lay?

Keeping a drake is only necessary if you are planning to breed. Otherwise, the ducks will lay quite happily without a male and, if you choose the right breed, provide almost one egg per day except during moulting periods.

Above All ducks enjoy swimming water. Provide a ramp for the ducks to use when getting in and out of a tub.

I don't have a stream or river – should I wait until I am able to move to a suitable situation before I keep ducks or geese?

No, you can keep most breeds of duck and goose straightaway as long as you have enough space for their run and are able to provide a large receptacle of water. All waterfowl need to be able to immerse their heads fully in water to keep their eyes clean, and also so they can splash to activate the preening gland. Most breeds do appreciate some swimming water, but this can be a small artificial pond – perhaps a child's rigid paddling pool or a more permanent arrangement. For the heavy ducks, water is a great aid to mating. The primary requirement for geese – although they do need some dipping and splashing water – is plenty of fresh grazing.

I've read about avian flu. Are waterfowl affected, and are they safe to keep?

Avian flu is a disease of birds, including waterfowl. There is a fear that it could mutate into a form that is contagious to humans, but the risk to waterfowl keepers is very low since domestic birds are kept away from our houses. Your state veterinary department can provide information on the disease and what steps you should take to keep your flock healthy. Because there is good awareness of the disease and each country has contingency plans to contain an outbreak promptly, avian flu is not present in our domestic flock. Nevertheless, all waterfowl keepers should familiarize themselves with their state veterinary recommendations and practise good bio-security.

I have a small orchard of around 0.1 ha (¼ acre). What breed and how many geese would keep it short, and would the fallen fruit be a hazard for them?

Geese are natural grazers and will keep your orchard well trimmed. Furthermore, they will positively enjoy any fallen fruit and eat it before it can attract insects or vermin. They will also let you know if anyone is in or near the orchard by honking loudly. You'll need to fence it well to keep them in, and decide if you are going to house them at night or make the whole orchard area predator-proof. You will also need to supply a large container of water. The area you have available could easily hold four or five geese but a pair or trio would be very happy, especially if the ground tends to become quite wet.

Muscovy ducks look more like geese. Should I treat them as geese or ducks?

The Muscovy is the only domestic duck that descends not from the Mallard but from a tree duck. It does behave differently but it is not a goose, despite the hissing noise it makes when alarmed. As with all duck breeds, it needs water in which to immerse its head, but is happy ranging on grass. It is also a particularly good flyer so you will need to clip the wings, although adult Muscovies have often been recorded as flying off during the day and returning home at night. Of course, it is safer if they remain on your property. As with all waterfowl, Muscovies are vulnerable to predators and especially if they have clipped wings and cannot fly. They are excellent mothers.

I've just bought a dozen ducklings from a sale. They are downy and I can't see any feathers. Do they need heat?
This is a surprisingly common question. It is sad to see young ducklings or goslings at sales, huddled together for warmth. In a warm summer they might just survive, but as they will be very tired and stressed from their ordeal it is always advisable to rig up a heat lamp in a draught-proof pen. Make sure they can get away from the heat source if they do get too hot, and that there is room for all of them underneath it if they need to warm up. You will have to work this out by trial and error, raising and lowering the lamp until the pen is warm but not overheated and the colder birds can find the heat source. Provide a shallow container of drinking water that they cannot fall in or tip over, soaking their downy feathers, and obtain duckling or chick crumbs as soon as you can. In an emergency, until you can obtain the balanced feed try grated hardboiled egg, greens or chopped nettles, and ground oats, barley or wheat mixed together. You should also complain to the sale organizers about their allowing ducklings or goslings to be offered for sale in unsuitable conditions.

I have a medium-sized garden with a pond. I didn't think I would be able to keep ducks, but someone told me there are bantam breeds. Will they damage my garden?
Yes, there are a number of delightful bantam duck breeds whose size alone makes them suitable for smaller areas. Having a pond will make them especially happy. Call

Left Call ducks (like these buff Call ducks) are great for smaller gardens ducks are ideal, but do note that their name represents their personality – they are very noisy and so not necessarily the best choice if you have near neighbours. The Miniature Silver Appleyard is an ornamental but productive choice, too. Unfortunately, no duck can distinguish weeds from flowers and inevitably garden plants will get damaged. On the plus side, in winter the ducks will do an excellent job of removing slugs and snails for the growing season. As with any livestock, a small number will do a lot less damage than a large flock, so you might find that a trio will be able to co-exist with your plants while also removing unwanted pests.

I've visited a poultry show and it looks like fun, but how experienced should I be before I enter one?

Your first step should be to join a local club and start showing in their members-only shows. Having said that, plenty of people have simply entered their nearest agricultural show 'for fun' and been very pleased with the results. The key is to show the best birds you have, and this all depends on the stock you have bought or bred. If you plan to show, go to an exhibitor/breeder and tell them that you intend to enter the birds in shows and breed for exhibition. The stock you are then offered will no doubt be more expensive but will form a good basis for competitive showing. Always make sure your birds are clean for competition and free from external parasites such as mite. All exhibitors agree that you never stop learning about waterfowl.

My duck is lame and appears to have a round swelling on her webs (feet). Will she recover?

It sounds as if your duck has bumble foot, a common but difficult-to-treat condition that affects webbed feet. It is nearly always caused by the bird treading on something sharp and the resulting small injury becoming infected. By the time the duck keeper notices it has usually become very infected, which is the swelling. Antibiotics and draining of the swelling might be appropriate and successful in some cases but by no means all, while some ducks may be able to live with it for many years. If treatment is unsuccessful or the lameness and swelling very exaggerated, humane slaughter may be the only solution. Prevention consists of removing any sharp stones in the area the ducks occupy and checking for glass or nails in paddock areas.

I'd like to breed from my geese. Should I take away the eggs to incubate or let them sit?

This depends on the breed of goose and the temperament of your birds. As geese form strong pair bonds they usually make very good parents, with the goose sitting to brood the eggs and the gander protectively watching over her. Most people would agree that when it is successful natural brooding is always easier than artificial, because the care of the young is left to the parents. However, it is advisable to learn as much as you can about natural brooding so that you can give support, or even remove the eggs to an incubator or goslings to a brooder if something goes badly wrong. If the goose is making a nest and trying to sit and her partner is behaving protectively, then take a chance and leave them to it. You will need to make sure that there is plenty of nutritious food nearby for the geese, the nest area is safe and dry, and predators cannot harm the goose. When the goslings have hatched, you will need to ensure their safety from predators – especially raptor-type birds – which will help the parent birds to care for their young.

Glossary

Abdomen The lower body of the bird.

Air space / air sac / Found at the broad end of the egg and seen by candling.

Ark A moveable house, shaped like an A. May have a run but normally too small for full-time confinement. Perches may have to be removed.

Albumen Egg-white.

Avian Flu (Bird flu) Notifiable bird disease with a high and low risk strain. Worldwide.

Bean Found on the beak of some ducks. Dark colored, raised, triangular patch.

Bill The upper and lower mandibles that form the mouth parts and is horny.

Breast Front of the bird's body.

Breed Club The governing body of each breed where enthusiasts and breeders share information and develop the standards. Membership usually open to all.

Breeding stock Selected adults to produce ducklings or goslings.

Broody A female bird who is preparing or sitting on eggs, characterized by vocal and physical defensive behavior when anyone approaches her nest. Also known as a clucker.

Brooders Artificial rearing units from small scale to commercial where a heat source replaces the bird to keep young birds warm.

Broodiness The maternal instinct of a broody bird.

Bumblefoot Caused by a sharp surface allowing infection into the webs.

Candling Looking through an egg, using a strong light, to check on the development of the embryo.

Carriage How the bird stands, an Indian Runner is upright for example, while other breeds may be more horizontal.

Caruncles Fleshy protuberances on the face of a Muscovy duck.

Coccidiostat Medication often contained in compound feeds to control the parasite coccidian.

Collar A band of color around the neck, often white or silver.

Compound feeds / concentrates Feed rations that are mixed and balanced for specific purposes such as ducklings, growers, breeders, adults, and finishers. Also known as bagged feed. Ensures the bird receives the correct nutrition for each stage of its life.

Coverts Small feathers on the wing and tail that surround the bases of the larger feathers.

Crossbred Matings across breeds resulting in no specific breed type.

Culling Removing (killing) inferior birds from the flock (sick, deformed, crippled birds to poor breed specimens). Must be done humanely.

Day-old A duckling or gosling up to 48 hours old.

Dead in shell The embryo has fully formed but been unable to hatch. Need to look at incubation methods if this happens often.

Dewlap A fold of skin, covered in feathers, that's hangs from the throat or gullet in some geese such as Toulouse.

Domestic breeds Birds developed for meat or eggs and often are docile and sociable. Many are nonflyers.

Down The fluffy feathers under the main feathers; of value to people for pillows and quilts.

Ducklings Young ducks until feathers have completely replaced their down.

Drake Male duck.

Duck A generic term but also used to denote a female duck.

Dummy eggs / pot eggs Pottery, wooden, or rubber eggs used to encourage broodiness or young birds to use a certain place to lay.

Flights The large feathers of the wings, including the primaries and secondaries; many people use this term to describe primaries only.

Fold unit Moveable house and run, more suitable for chickens but can be of use for ducklings or goslings to keep them safe from predators.

Free range Where birds are allowed to range over an area with low stocking rates but confined at night against predators. Often used incorrectly where large flocks range over comparatively small areas.

Frizzle Curled or twisted feathers; once accidental and now encouraged in certain breeds.

Gander Male goose.

Gizzard Muscular organ that grinds the food eaten by birds and requires grit in order to function.

Goose Generic term but also used to denote a female goose.

Goslings Young geese until feathers have completely replaced their down.

Hatching The process of the fully formed embryo, now a duckling or gosling, breaking out of the egg shell. A good hatch refers to a high percentage of the incubated eggs successfully hatching.

Hybrid Carefully selected genetics from pure breeds commercially bred to become a high egg-layer or meat producer.

Inbred Closely related birds e.g. brother to sister. Can cause genetic problems or emphasize genetic faults.

Infra-red Type of heat bulb for providing heat for young birds – ideally should be dull so it is not 24 hour daylight.

Keel The ridge along the breast bone; the fold of skin suspended from the sternum (underneath the bird).

Knob A fleshy protuberance on the forehead of geese descended from the swan geese.

Lobes The folds of skin that hang from the abdomen on many geese, can be one or two and are described as single or dual lobed.

Mash Confusingly, mash is often dry and it is ground poultry compound or concentrate food. Fed dry to chickens but must be damp for waterfowl and therefore soon becomes sour if not eaten.

Molt The shedding of old feathers and replacing with new; the replacement of feathers for courtship display. Waterfowl need to be well fed during this stressful period.

Paunch Pendulous folds below the lower abdomen.

Pin feathers Newly emerging feathers after a molt. Makes plucking ducks after a certain age very difficult.

Plucking Removal of feathers from a dead bird in preparation for cooking – can be done dry or wet – advantages and disadvantages for both.

Primaries The ten main flight feathers on a wing.

Preening Lubricating feathers from the preening gland situated at the base of the rump. Waterfowl need to be wet to do this and so need access to splashing water at least.

Preen gland Situated at the base of the tail and produces the oil needed for preening.

Purebred A specific breed that has no cross-breds for many generations.

Quill The stem of a feather, once used for writing with ink.

Secondaries Inner flight feathers.

Sex curls The curls in a drake's tail that shows maleness.

Shaft Central stem of the feather.

Slipped wing "Wing in which the primary feathers hang below the secondaries when the wing is closed" British Poultry Standards. Also known as Angel Wing.

Speculum Iridescent secondary feathers of the mallard, the blue mark on the drake.

Stern The area below the tail, around the vent.

Strain A particular line that has been selected for certain characteristics such as egg laying over many generations.

Standards / standard bred Waterfowl that have been selected to meet the breed standards according to each country's specification.

Standard of Perfection (in USA) / Poultry Club Standards / "Blue book" in UK Detailed descriptions and photos in a book of the perfect breed example as agreed by each breed club.

Tertiaries Feathers attached to the wing bone closest to the body and overlaying the secondaries.

Trio A group of one male and two females. Often birds are sold like this.

Table birds Waterfowl more suitable for the table than egg laying, more usually heard in chickens.

Type The shape of a bird e.g. boxy or slim.

Utility A purebreed that is recognized for egg laying or meat production but often taken to mean a bird that can provide reasonable amounts of both products. Very popular pre- and immediately post-World War II until intensive rearing systems brought about the development of hybrids.

Web The skin between the toes that form the webs (feet) of waterfowl.

Vent The rear opening of the digestive tract and the oviduct where waste and eggs are passed.

Waterfowl Birds that would naturally spend much of their time on water such as ducks, geese, and swans.

Wildfowl Often known as Ornamental. Breeds that exist in the wild usually kept in wildfowl collections and need specialist care. They characteristically are more timid than domestic breeds and are good flyers. Not kept for egg laying or meat.

Wry back Twisted spine.

Wry tail Tail is out of line with the back bone.

Acknowledgements

Acknowledgements

T.F.H. Publications
President/CEO Glen S. Axelrod
Executive Vice President Mark E. Johnson
Publisher Christopher T. Reggio
Production Manager Kathy Bontz
US Editor Craig Sernotti

T.F.H. Publications, Inc.
One TFH Plaza
Third and Union Avenues
Neptune City, NJ 07753

Special thanks to Janice Houghton Wallace, *Smallholder* Magazine, Valerie Charlesworth, all the exhibitors in the Poultry Fancy who have taught me so much – and that you carry on learning all your life, *Fancy Fowl* Magazine, David Bland, Christopher Marler, the Ashtons, and all the wise men and women whose books from the past have given me such an insight into the waterfowl world of years gone by.

Picture Acknowledgements

Main photography © Octopus Publishing Group Ltd/Mick Corrigan.

Other Photography:
11, 12 poultryphotos.co.uk; 23 Parkland Products; 39 Paul Hobson/nplibrary.com; 70 Jason Bye/Rex Features; 71 Jamie McDonald/Getty Images; 81, 83 Peter Dean/Agripicture.com; 88 Philippe Clement/nplibrary.com; 113 poultryphotos.co.uk; 120 Don Hadden/Ardea; 123 Frank W Lane/FLPA; 136 Arco Images/Alamy; 174 R P Lawrence/FLPA; 180 Ruth Grimes/Alamy; 196 David Harrison/Natural Visions.